What people are saying about *Amazing Faith*...

"Leaders who make bold moves for God's Kingdom inspire me. Wilfredo De Jesús and New Life Covenant Church exemplify amazing faith in ways worth emulating."

Bill Hybels

Senior Pastor, Willow Creek Community Church

Chairman of Board, Willow Creek Association

"In my work with pastors and churches, I always appreciate those who seem to be captured by God's heart. Pastor Choco is one of those people. I've had the privilege to watch God use him to touch lives in his neighborhood, in the city of Chicago, across our country, and around the world. But the broad scope of his work isn't the most significant thing about him. Pastor Choco passionately loves Jesus Christ. His book is a chronicle of men and women in the Bible who had amazing faith, and he inspires all the people he meets to trust God with every fiber of their being. Read this book. It will enflame your love for God and point you to touch the lives of others."

Dr. George O. Wood

General Superintendent of the Assemblies of God

Springfield, Missouri

"It has been my pleasure to know Pastor Wilfredo De Jesús as one of the foremost spiritual leaders in America. He is a man who chooses right over wrong, ethics over convenience, and truth over popularity. I highly recommend to you his latest book *Amazing Faith*. It will challenge every believer to expand their faith to higher heights and deeper depths."

Pastor John Hagee

Cornerstone Church

San Antonio, Texas

"I've known Choco for many years as a pastor who is deeply committed to his community and growing congregation. He knows that if the Gospel is to transform his neighborhood, his people will have to reach out to prostitutes, drug addicts and the poor who have no place to call home.

This is the story of an unlikely boy, called by God to give visionary leadership to one of Chicago's most needy communities. These pages have increased my own faith and given me a greater burden for a world that has lost its way. If you want to be inspired, convicted and motivated to do more for the cause of the Gospel read this book and pass it along to a friend."

Dr. Erwin Lutzer

The Moody Church

Chicago

"C.S. Lewis once said 'If you cannot turn language to the vernacular, you either don't believe it or don't understand it.' Pastor Choco gets it! He believes it, understands it and lives it! His amazing stories interpret the amazing grace of God in a lost world. In this book you will see the beauty of a grass-root movement that focuses on being the church 'from below.' Here is compassion in action by a young Hispanic Pentecostal preacher in the context of the current social and spiritual situation of America's cities. This is deep theology in the dialect of the shallow and hopeless 21st century culture. Read it!"

Dr. Jesse Miranda

Founder and President

The Jesse Miranda Center for Hispanic Leadership

"*Amazing Faith* is an amazing book written by an amazing leader, Wilfredo De Jesús. *Amazing Faith* will inspire you with one man's amazing courage for a community that is fueled by an amazing passion for the lost that results in amazing stories of life change. *Amazing Faith* is easy to read but a challenge to live out. If you are satisfied with the status quo, then don't read this book; but if you want to have an amazing faith of your own, read it now!"

Dave Ferguson

Lead Pastor, Community Christian Church

Spiritual Entrepreneur, NewThing

"As a Christian leader I'm always aware of one key component to effective ministry . . . Passion!!! Passion gets you out of bed in the morning, keeps you up late into the midnight hours, and energizes you when you don't think you can stay awake one more minute. As you read this book, you will encounter a 'Man of God' so full of passion for people that tears will begin to flow down your own cheeks. Get ready to be changed."

Rich Wilkerson

Senior Pastor, Trinity Church

Founder, Peacemakers

"When the footsteps of my destiny crossed the path of Pastor Wilfredo, I found him standing firm on the foundation of his "Amazing Faith." I have watched him transcend from having one of the most powerful youth ministries in the city of Chicago to a church that holistically ministers to the masses worldwide. Pastor Wilfredo's journey from humble beginnings to biblical prosperity emphatically testifies of what is possible when hard work brings your faith to life. This book is guaranteed to stretch you to walk on water, part the Red Sea, and fulfill God's original intent of exposing the greatness that is within you. Faith without works is dead! I promise you that after reading *Amazing Faith,* all of your dreams will resurrect and manifest. Get ready to be all that God has called you to be by using your God-given measure of amazing faith."

John Hannah
Senior Pastor, New Life Covenant Southeast

"Amazing Faith is a phenomenal compilation of faith biographies of some of the Bible's most notable figures. As you read it, you will be literally fueled with faith."

Charles Jenkins
Senior Pastor of Fellowship Missionary Baptist Church and
founder of Relevant Forums
Chicago

"This book directly corresponds to the character of our father: powerful, honest and encouraging."

Alex, Yesenia and Pito

WILFREDO DE JESÚS

FOREWORD BY RICK WARREN

AMAZING FAITH

HOW TO MAKE GOD TAKE NOTICE

InfluenceResources.com

Published by Influence Resources
1445 N. Boonville Ave., Springfield, Missouri 65802

Published in association with The Quadrivium Group—Orlando, FL
info@TheQuadriviumGroup.com

Cover design and interior formatting by Anne McLaughlin of
Blue Lake Design, Dickinson, Texas
Edited by Stan Campbell, Hendersonville, Tennessee

Unless otherwise specified, Scripture quotations are taken from The Holy Bible, New International Version® NIV®. Copyright © 1973, 1978, 1984, 2011 by Biblica, Inc.™ Used by permission. All rights reserved.

Note: In some of the stories in this book, the names and details have been changed to protect anonymity.

ISBN: 978-1-93669-995-7
First printing 2012
Second printing 2013
Third printing 2013

Printed in the United States of America

To the woman who was my girlfriend, who became my wife and the mother of my children, and who is the first lady of our church with a heart of worship. I dedicate this book to you, Elizabeth De Jesús.

Contents

Acknowledgements

This book is the product of God's grace and the love of many people who have poured themselves into my life. The Lord has been gracious and merciful to me. For that and so much more, I want to acknowledge my Father in heaven, my friend and counselor. Thank you, Jesus.

I also want to thank . . .

My wife, Elizabeth and our three gifts, Alexandria, Yesenia, and Wilfredo. You mean the world to me. Thank you for always believing in me.

My mom, who raised me as a single mother. I will always remember your faithfulness toward God and your family. And to my siblings, thank you for all your support in my endeavors.

My father-in-law and my mother-in-law. Thank you for trusting me. Your confidence means the world to me.

My gifted and wonderful staff at our church. Your loyalty and dedication—to God, to our church, and to me—are always an inspiration to me.

My friends. You have been with me for over 30 years, and together, God is using us to change the world. I love you so much.

My church family at New Life Covenant. Words cannot express my appreciation for your support for me and my family. In every situation, you have shown me an amazing amount of grace as I've tried to lead and serve you.

My editor Pat Springle. You are the first editor I've ever met, and in my view, the very best. I appreciate your professionalism and patience throughout this process. Thank you for helping me put into words what was in my heart.

My assistant on this book project, Ibelisse Sánchez-Sanders. Thank you for the hours of reading and proofing. I would be kidding myself if I thought I could have done that on my own. I appreciate you.

Foreword

In *Amazing Faith*, Wilfredo De Jesús, better known as "Pastor Choco," shares the testimonies of ordinary people with extraordinary faith. The Bible makes it clear that Christians are to live by faith, yet most Christians don't even have a working definition of authentic faith in God. The Bible says, "Without faith it is impossible to please God." God is pleased when His children put their trust in Him. In fact, faith is so important that God gives us many examples throughout the Scriptures, including Abraham, Gideon, Noah, Moses, Rahab, and many more.

In *Amazing Faith* you will read the stories of everyday people, just like the men and women of the Bible, who risked having faith in God despite the pain they suffered. The fact is—God uses pain in our lives to get our attention. We don't change when we see *the light*; we change when we feel *the heat*. God allows pain to teach you to depend on Him. In the book of Psalms, David wrote, "My suffering was good for me, for it taught me to pay attention to your decrees." There are things we will learn only through pain because we, as flawed humans, are too stubborn to learn it otherwise.

God also allows pain in your life to give you a ministry to others. The testimonies of *Amazing Faith* are of wounded people who are now sharing their wisdom, using their great faith in God to help build the faith of others. Who can better help an alcoholic than somebody who struggled with alcoholism? Who can better help somebody dealing with the pain of abuse than a former victim of brutality? God wants to use and recycle the pain in your life to help others, but you've got to be open and honest about it. If you keep your hurt to yourself, you're wasting it.

My prayer is that you and your small group will be inspired, challenged, and reignited by the stories of *Amazing Faith*. God wants to use the pain in your life to help others. There is no greater reward, no greater joy, and no greater satisfaction than helping somebody find and experience Christ's transforming grace. God wants to use you and your story for His purpose. Take a risk, have faith in God, and He will do amazing things you never thought possible.

God Bless You!

Rick Warren

Founding Pastor, Saddleback Church

Introduction: Ordinary People, Extraordinary Faith

If Christ lives in us, controlling our personalities, we will leave glorious marks on the lives we touch. Not because of our lovely characters, but because of his.

—Eugenia Price

No one is beyond the transforming power of God's love. No one is too lost, too evil, too wounded, or too hopeless. In the pages of the New Testament, we see Jesus reaching out to touch the lives of pitiful prostitutes and arrogant, power-hungry leaders. He loved the most obscure, despised leper as well as rich, corrupt tax collectors. He showed His mercy to the down-and-outers and the up-and-comers. No one was off limits. The Bible tells an amazing story of God's open arms that welcome anyone who responds, but the story didn't end on the last page of the Bible. God still changes lives.

When I was eight years old, my mother told me that my dad was going to leave her and her six kids. He was an alcoholic who owned a bar in Humboldt Park in Chicago. As soon as she told me the painful news, I ran to the bar to beg my father to stay. Somehow, the tears and pleading of his little boy didn't make any difference to him. When I walked out that day, I had a sick, empty feeling. I had no idea what this would mean for my mother and the rest of us, but I knew it would bring plenty of heartaches.

The next few months and years were a blur of trying desperately to make life work. My mother found a number of dead-end jobs to try to earn money, but we were on welfare much of the time. We had to move several times, and I had to change schools each time. People probably thought we were Gypsies instead of Puerto Ricans. Dad left a gaping hole in our lives—emotionally and financially. I felt angry, confused, and anxious. Every day, survival was our driving goal. Mom was incredibly brave, but she couldn't mask her uncertainty. To help her, I got a job after school at a corner grocery store cleaning floors and stocking shelves. Sometimes my friends came in, and I sold them some candy. I didn't make much, but I knew even a few dollars would help my mother.

My older brothers tried to take Dad's place of leadership in our home, but they were just kids. Humboldt Park was infested with gangs, and soon, they joined one of them.

When I was twelve, the Hispanic community in Humboldt Park finally became fed up with the brutality and prejudice of the police. Furious people rioted for three long, bloody days. Gangs roamed the streets overturning and burning cars, throwing rocks at police, and breaking into buildings to loot stores. The police clamped down and shot a number of people. Each night I hoped the violence would stop, but it returned the next morning. The police weren't able to control the situation, so the governor sent in the National Guard. Our community had become a war zone.

On the second day of the riot, I was with a crowd standing in front of a grocery store. Someone broke the front window, and people ran in to take anything they wanted. They carried out cases of food. I was caught up in the moment, but I could bring myself only to steal a bottle of soda pop from the refrigerator. I walked outside into the chaos of paddy wagons, burning cars, and people running. I walked a few steps

down the street to get away, and
then I stopped dead in my tracks. I
thought, What in the world am I doing? I knew it was wrong to steal, so
I turned around, went back into the
free-for-all at the store, and put the
bottle back on the refrigerator shelf.

What's wrong with me? People are rioting and looting, but I can't even steal a single bottle of soda pop! Who am I, anyway?

When I walked outside again, I didn't feel relieved. More than ever, I
was confused and conflicted. I wondered, *What's wrong with me? People
are rioting and looting, but I can't even steal a single bottle of soda pop! Who
am I, anyway?*

The riots finally stopped, but the bitterness remained. My brothers
were furious with the police, and my mother felt more vulnerable than
ever. I didn't know where I belonged. I didn't want to join my brothers
in their gang, but I knew I couldn't make it on my own.

Two years later I got a job in a Chicago summer youth program.
Mayor Richard J. Daley set up a program to keep kids busy and clean up
the streets. I was eager to make some money, so I signed up. Each community had a hub where the kids showed up for their assignments. I was
told to go to an Assemblies of God church. Every morning when I arrived at the church to get my directions for the day, I saw a group of kids
praying at the altar. I stayed in the back. Our family hadn't been particularly religious, but I was familiar enough with church to know their
behavior wasn't normal! They were my age, but they weren't acting like
anyone I knew. As they prayed, they obviously felt very passionately
about something. They weren't traditional and formal like the churches
I'd attended. They hugged each other, prayed out loud, and lifted their
hands. It was strange . . . but very intriguing.

I could tell these kids really loved each other, and I soon realized they loved me. It felt like a family—the kind of family my mother was trying desperately to provide but which had proven elusive. After a few days observing these kids, the supervisor noticed my interest. He smiled and asked, "Do you know Jesus?"

I wasn't sure what he meant. I knew about Jesus, but I wasn't aware it was possible to know Him like I knew other people. I think I said, "Yes, I know Him," but he could tell I was confused.

He asked, "Do you want to trust in Jesus and have Him live in your heart?"

I must have said something that resembled "Yes," so he called the kids over and asked them to pray for me. They gathered around me and formed a circle. Instantly, I was on edge. I was no fool. In Humboldt Park, people are put in the center of a circle only in gang initiations, and the one being inducted is often beaten as a rite of passage. The kids came in close around me, but I kept my eyes open to see if any fists or bats were coming my way. If anybody raised his hand, I was going to punch him in the face!

Everyone wants to belong to someone or something.

The love of those young people melted my heart. In a few minutes, I prayed to accept Jesus as my Savior, and my life changed forever. Don't get me wrong. I had a lot to learn about life and God, and there were a lot of sinful patterns of behavior that needed to be changed. But I'd begun a relationship with the God of the universe, and I'd found a family I could call my own. In the most important ways, everything was different for me.

Everyone wants to belong to someone or something. My brothers belonged to a gang, but now I belonged to a family of loving people. In a city full of gangs, belonging to a group means you stand up for them, defend them, and represent them. It's not just about you anymore; your identity is tied up in the group's purpose. For the next several years, gangbangers often stopped me on the street and asked, "Hey, what you be about?"

If I'd said "nothing," they would either beat me up or try to recruit me. I looked them in the eye and said confidently, "I represent Jesus Christ. What you be about?"

They might answer with a swagger, "Latin Kings," or "Disciples," or another gang in our community. Because I belonged to a group and represented it with pride, they shook my hand and went on their way.

In a community like ours, the only way young people earn respect is by affiliating with a group whose members back each other. Several of us who attended church together realized we were acting like a gang—representing our leader and defending each other—so we decided to make it official. We became the Jesus gang. On several occasions, we came out of church and were surrounded by gangs carrying bats and chains. These weren't singers in *West Side Story*. The threat of getting our heads smashed in was very real. Invariably, one of them snarled, "What you be about?"

Without blinking an eye, we answered proudly, "We represent Jesus." That's all they needed to hear. If we showed weakness, they'd have pounced on us with full fury. But our confidence caused them to back off. They respected our boldness.

We were thoroughly ordinary people. We had no advanced degrees and no amazing talents, but we were convinced that we belonged to God and to each other. God gave us extraordinary faith to cling to Him and to see ourselves as His representatives in Humboldt Park. From the beginning, I knew that trusting in Jesus had caused a paradigm shift in my life. I no longer represented only myself or my mom. I now stood for someone far bigger and more important: Jesus Christ. And now, I wasn't just a number in a national census. God had given me an important role in His kingdom. My role, though, wasn't any different from the one He gives every believer: to stand tall for Him and make a difference in our communities.

I was a young man who longed for a purpose bigger than myself, and I found it. I suspect I'm not alone. God has put it in the heart of every person to long for more . . . much more than a dull, ordinary life. Riches, power, and honor promise to fill the gaping hole in our hearts, but they can't. We soon realize we're as empty as ever. Only Jesus Christ truly satisfies. And we're never alone. When the kids circled around me to pray for me at that little church, God gave me a new family. From that day, the family of God has been my home. In this family, everything we are and everything we do represents Jesus, and we want to represent Him well—in our homes, in our businesses, on the streets, at the park, as well as in our churches. We belong to Him all day every day, and together, we can make a difference.

People who saw a confused kid take the bottle of soda pop back into the looted store during a riot would likely have asked, "Can anything good come out of that boy's life?" It was a valid question, and at the time, the answer was still up in the air. The same question could be asked of the nine people we'll encounter in these chapters, including a pagan prostitute who had no background in the faith and no interest in God, a Roman officer whose emperor demanded complete and undivided loyalty, a poor widow who had almost nothing but gave everything, and an arrogant Jew who despised Jesus and His people. Can God do anything with these people? Yes, He could and He did. Can He do anything with you and me? Of course He can.

No one is beyond Christ's reach—including the people who live under our roofs, the people we work with each day, the people we walk past without giving them a second thought, and you and me. When He touches our lives, He gives us a purpose far bigger than the pursuit of comfort, riches, and acclaim. He gives us the high honor of representing Him to everyone—those who are threatening, people who are cool, and the ones who are apathetic. Each of us has a past, but we don't have to be defined by our past any longer. The forgiveness Christ offers transforms us, and we no longer let the past dictate our future.

No one is beyond Christ's reach—including the people who live under our roofs, the people we work with each day, the people we walk past without giving them a second thought, and you and me.

We often talk about how God is amazing to us, and we sing songs like "Amazing Grace." On several occasions, the Gospel writers turn this around and mention that the faith of a few people amazed Jesus. But also, He was occasionally amazed by the lack of faith exhibited by people who should have been convinced He could do anything. A life of faith isn't easy. It requires everything we've got. If we put ourselves in God's hands without reservation, He gives us blessings far more valuable than all the wealth people pursue. The missionary Jim Elliott captured this promise when he wrote in his journal, "He is no fool who gives what he cannot keep to gain what he cannot lose."[1] Amazing faith gives us insight and courage to give away things that seem so important to most people—possessions, positions, and power—but ultimately,

---

1   Cited in Elisabeth Elliott's *Through Gates of Splendor* (Harper & Brothers: New York, 1958), 172.

they are things that don't matter at all. When we surrender those things, God fills our hearts with His love, strength, and purpose, and we become complete.

As you read this book, I hope you are both inspired and disturbed. I trust God will use His Word to convince you that His grace is the most wonderful experience in life, but you can be sure that feeling loved and comfortable isn't His ultimate aim for us. We belong to Him, and we represent Him to everyone we meet. Peter described our identity and purpose: "But you are a chosen people, a royal priesthood, a holy nation, God's special possession, that you may declare the praises of him who called you out of darkness into his wonderful light" (1 Peter 2:9).

The grace of God makes us feel wonderfully warm and safe, but God never intended us to stay there. We have the privilege to "declare His praises" in everything we say and do. We love the unlovely because we've experienced God's amazing love. We stand up strong to honor Him because Jesus bowed low to pay the ultimate price for us. Our hearts are filled with His Spirit—not for our sakes, but to inspire us to touch the lives of those around us.

Sir Francis Drake was one of the most daring captains in the Age of Discovery. He was among the first to sail around the world. However, few people realize his true motivation. In a powerful and beautiful prayer, he explained:

> Disturb us, Lord, when we are too well pleased with ourselves, when our dreams have come true because we have dreamed too little, when we arrive safely because we sailed too close to the shore.

> Disturb us, Lord, when with the abundance of things we possess, we have lost our thirst for the waters of life, having fallen

in love with life, we have ceased to dream of eternity, and in our efforts to build a new earth, we have allowed our vision of the new heaven to dim.

Disturb us, Lord, to dare more boldly, to venture on wider seas, where storms will show your mastery, where losing sight of land, we shall find the stars. We ask you to push back the horizon of our hopes, and to push us into the future in strength, courage, hope, and love. This we ask in the name of our Captain, who is Jesus Christ.[2]

This is my prayer for you as you read this book. Believe big. Dream big. Represent the King of kings with boldness and joy.

By the way, my friends and people at our church call me "Pastor Choco." You might wonder how I got this name. When I was young, my family, particularly my uncle, called me "Chocolate" (pronounced cho-co-LAH-tay in Spanish) because of my love for sweets and chocolate. When I began attending church, the youth must have found my nickname to be too long because soon it was just "Choco." That's how I'm known today.

One more thing: At the end of each chapter, you'll find a few questions designed to stimulate personal reflection and group discussion. Too often, people read a chapter of a book and put it down without wrestling with the principles. Don't let that happen! Take some time to think, write, and pray over the questions. If you're in a class or small

---

2   Sir Francis Drake, 1577. Cited by John H. Armstrong in *Your Church Is Too Small* (Zondervan: Grand Rapids, 2010), 191.

group, use these questions to guide your discussion. I hope your conversations will be rich, and I trust God will use your discussions to build your faith so strong that it amazes Him.

1   A Most Unlikely Source

Real Christians are marked by sincerity—the whole truth about themselves and the whole truth about God. Real Christians stand before people the way they stand before God—transparent and vulnerable. Anything less is a dressed-up Gospel.

—John Fischer

The first time I saw Marisol, her eyes were lifeless. She'd been selling her body for years, using heroin to numb the pain. She remembers, "I had been a functioning addict. I had a job, and I had my kids. I earned enough money to pay the bills and get high, but when I needed more to get the same effect, I ran out of money. A friend told me she knew a way I could make some easy money. I was going through withdrawals, so I was desperate to get enough money to get high again. She took me to a particular street in the city, and she told me, 'Just stand here and look pretty. Somebody will pick you up.' That's exactly what happened. At the time I still looked healthy, so the guys were glad to find me."

Marisol made good money as a prostitute, so she spent more time on the street. Soon, she lost her regular job. Every day she walked the streets to find a john so she could make enough money for her next hit. Her only relationships were with the men who used her and walked away, and with other prostitutes who saw her as competition. She felt utterly alone.

Like many prostitutes, Marisol had become sexually active as a young girl. Her stepfather and several other men had abused her, and she learned to equate sex with love. She had an insatiable desire to feel wanted, so she found herself in bed with all kinds of men. Drugs soon followed. When her friend told her she could make some money for drugs by hiring herself out for a few minutes, it seemed like a logical and necessary step. It was easy, and the money was good, so she got hooked on the lifestyle. But she paid a price. When respectable people passed her on the street, they looked the other way. She was damaged goods, and they didn't want to have anything to do with her. They were sure she must have STDs, so they wanted to stay as far away as possible. She knew it, and it hurt. Her loneliness only increased.

Marisol had two children, but when she became too engrossed in drugs and sex to care for them, her parents took over their care. Whenever she let herself feel anything, she suffered from intense, gnawing shame. Her life was a disaster, but she saw no way out. She told herself that she didn't care—about her kids, about her parents, about the men who used her, or about herself. As her mental and physical condition deteriorated, she became less attractive to men, so her value diminished. She had to turn more tricks for less money. Staying numb was the only way she could cope with the intense pain and loneliness.

When Marisol came through the door of our church, she was emaciated because she hadn't eaten in days. She had spent every dime on drugs. Her face was pale, and her expression was empty. She looked more like a corpse than a human being. I tried to talk to her, but she was very suspicious. It had been years since a man talked to her without a sexual agenda. I tried to make eye contact, but she looked down the whole time. I told her I wanted to help her, but I immediately realized a thousand guys had told her the same thing. No wonder she was suspicious of me. I sensed, though, that this was a holy moment. I asked, "Do you want to dream again? It's not what you've lost—it's what you have left. Give all you are and all you have to God and see what happens."

> Give all you are and all you have to God and see what happens.

Carmen, one of our pastors, told Marisol that God loved her and could restore her life. Marisol had heard about God before, but she couldn't comprehend the promise of forgiveness and restoration. She recalls, "I was convinced I was nothing but a five-dollar prostitute, and I'd never be anything else. I was sure this was the way life would always be." But Carmen didn't take "No" for an answer. She laid hands on Marisol and prayed for her. She claimed Marisol for Christ and trusted God to work a miracle.

OVER THE WALL

Over 3000 years ago, another prostitute was in a crisis. Four decades earlier, Moses had led God's people out of Egypt. God wanted to take them to the Promised Land in Canaan, and Moses had sent out twelve spies to see what it would take to conquer the land. Ten of them returned with bad news: There were giants there who would crush the invasion. Two other spies, Joshua and Caleb, gave a very different report. They said it would be difficult, but God had promised to deliver the country into their hands. They were ready to go!

The people, however, sided with the fearful ten. God wasn't pleased with their unbelief. He let them wander in the desert for forty years until the generation of doubters had died—all but Joshua and Caleb. By the time they approached the Jordan River to cross it and enter the land, Joshua was their new leader. Like Moses had done, Joshua sent spies ahead, this time to the city of Jericho. The two men disguised themselves and went into a house, probably an inn, where a prostitute named Rahab had set up shop. The two men hadn't watched many detective movies, so they didn't know how to blend in with a crowd of strangers. Rahab attempted to hide them on her roof under stacks of drying flax. (She must have been quite a businesswoman. She had at least two businesses.) She had heard of Israel's God and believed in Him, and she wanted to protect the spies. But their cover had already been blown. The king of Jericho sent soldiers to Rahab. They knocked on her door and demanded, "Where are the spies?"

At that moment, Rahab faced a stark choice. I can imagine her looking at the faces of the soldiers, then thinking of the two spies on her roof. *Hmmm. Which will it be? Do I betray my country or betray my new faith?*

A prostitute learns to be skilled in telling lies. An angry wife may show up at her door and ask, "Is my husband in there?" She smiles and shrugs, "I don't know your husband. What does he look like? If I see him, I'll tell him to go home."

An army captain may come to her and demand, "Have you seen my men? Turn them over to me right now!" She tells him, "I don't know about them, but I'm available for you right now."

Rahab had probably lied countless times, so she deceived the soldiers at her door. She told them the men of Israel had been there, but that they had left and headed back across the Jordan. The king's men bought her line and left immediately to look for them. When Rahab shut the door behind the departing soldiers, she was closing the door on everything she had known in life. She knew that when they eventually found out she had lied to them, she would have nowhere to hide.

By the way, some people have big problems with Rahab's lying to the king's men. Give her a break. She had only believed in God for a short time. Some of us have been Christians for years, and we still struggle. The Jewish spies on the roof may have heard parts of the conversation at the front door, and then they heard footsteps on the stairs. They strained to determine if it was a woman or a squad of soldiers. When Rahab appeared, they were relieved to know their heads would stay attached to their bodies. She wasn't suddenly being gracious to strangers. She had a very different motive for her actions. She'd heard stories about God's power and His promise to deliver her land into the hands of God's people—and she believed every word. When she climbed back to the roof to tell the men they were safe, she explained,

> **She'd heard stories about God's power and His promise to deliver her land into the hands of God's people—and she believed every word.**

> "I know that the LORD has given you this land and that a great fear of you has fallen on us, so that all who live in this country are melting in fear because of you. We have heard how the LORD dried up the water of the Red Sea for you when you came out of Egypt, and what you did to Sihon and Og, the two kings of the Amorites east of the Jordan, whom you completely destroyed. When we heard of it, our hearts melted in fear and everyone's courage failed because of you, for the LORD your God is God in heaven above and on the earth below" (Joshua 2:9-11).

Rahab was a pagan woman. She had no heritage of faith in the true God, but she'd heard convincing stories that the God of the Israelites was powerful—and the Israelites were coming! Part of the story she'd heard happened decades before, but other amazing events had occurred very recently. She could have dismissed them as wild rumors, or she could believe them and take action. We sense the intensity in her voice as she made a deal with the men on the roof:

> "Now then, please swear to me by the Lord that you will show kindness to my family, because I have shown kindness to you. Give me a sure sign that you will spare the lives of my father and mother, my brothers and sisters, and all who belong to them— and that you will save us from death" (Joshua 2:12-13).

In spite of her life of prostitution, she still cared for her family—she still had the spark of humanity in her. Her family may have given up on her, and they may have despised her—but she wanted to be a channel of salvation to them.

The spies were in no position to haggle. They immediately agreed to the deal and told her, "Our lives for your lives! If you don't tell what we are doing, we will treat you kindly and faithfully when the LORD gives us the land" (Joshua 2:14).

Rahab's house was on the wall of the city, so she helped the men escape by lowering them out of her window. She knew the search patterns of the army. (She must have gotten plenty of information from her customers.) She gave the spies instructions about how to prevent capture. In return, they told her to tie a scarlet cord outside her window and invite her whole family to her home when she heard the invasion was underway. She agreed, and they left. When the spies gave their report to Joshua, they told him, "The LORD has surely given the whole

land into our hands; all the people are melting in fear because of us"
(Joshua 2:24).

In one of the most miraculous and memorable events in the Bible, God gave His people a very strange battle plan: Blow trumpets
and march around the city for seven days. During those days, God's
people walked, waited, and worshiped. What were Rahab's parents
and siblings thinking during that time? Did Rahab tell them the whole
story? I doubt it. She was probably afraid one of them would freak
out on the fourth day of the musical
siege and tell the king! When the
walls of the city fell on the seventh
day, the invading army rescued Rahab and her family.

Rahab was a most unlikely
candidate to change the course of
history. Who would have imagined that God's divine purposes for His
people would rest on the faith of a woman of the street? When the
spies needed a person they could trust, God led them to Rahab's house.
When their cover was blown and they faced capture, torture, and death,
she protected them. When they could have been caught on the way
back to their army, she gave them detailed information to help them
evade Jericho's soldiers. Her efforts were instrumental in opening the
door to the Promised Land. We need to remember that Rahab wasn't
exactly a seminary graduate. Her faith was strong, but it was based on
stories passed down for generations. She didn't have the Scriptures, and
she didn't have a church where she could hear messages of truth. But
she responded in amazing faith to the truth she had.

Elements in Rahab's story point us backward and forward. Gathering her family under one roof to escape death is reminiscent of another

> Who would have imagined that God's divine purposes for His people would rest on the faith of a woman of the street?

night, forty years earlier, when God told His people to get their families together while the Angel of Death killed the firstborn children in Egypt. The scarlet cord at her window reminds us of the lambs' blood on the doorposts and lintels of the homes that night. The red rope also points us to the future. It symbolizes the blood of Jesus that saves us from sin and death, just as the red rope saved Rahab and her family from the attack by God's army.

But there's even more to Rahab's story. After the walls of Jericho fell, she married an Israelite and became the great-great-grandmother of King David. When Matthew records the genealogy of the Messiah in his Gospel, he includes Rahab in the lineage of Jesus (Matthew 1:5). A woman who might have been considered a throwaway became an ancestor of the Savior of the world. The writer of Hebrews includes her in the Hall of Fame (Hebrews 11:31), and James uses her as a primary example of strong, vibrant, living faith (James 2:25). Can God change a flawed person's identity and destiny? Yes, look at Rahab.

FOLLOWING HER EXAMPLE

Stories of great *faith* are invariably stories of great *grace*. Rahab trusted the truth she had been given, and God flung open the doors of heaven to bless her and her family. She didn't have a ton of written material or excellent teachers to help her. She'd heard stories about God doing miracles—some long ago and some recently—but they were enough.

What does it take to convince you and me? Do we need a mountain of evidence before we believe? I know people who refuse to trust God even when they've witnessed His power to transform lives and they've heard years of messages from the Bible. For most of us, the problem isn't the depth of our theology but the humility of our hearts. Today we have the Internet, television programs, and all kinds of ways to hear authentic stories of changed lives. Sure, some of the things out there are phony, but many are rich and real. When we hear them, we might think, *Well, that's great for them, but my situation is different.* No, it's not! If God can work in their lives—and in a Jericho prostitute's life—He can work in ours, too. Rahab teaches us several important lessons.

Rahab didn't let her past dictate her future.

She had been used and abused by men in her life. She could have felt sorry for herself, and she could have blamed everyone—including God—for her life being an empty wreck. But she wasn't willing to remain stuck in a dead-end life. When the time came to make a choice and take God's hand, she took it. Her decision wasn't easy. It was full of life-threatening risks, but she found the courage to make a clear choice, accept the risks, and trust that God would fulfill His promises.

Plenty of people are paralyzed by fear and resentment. They've suffered cruelly from parents, spouses, bosses, and friends. The hurt is palpable and ever-present. Sadly, they've developed a victim mentality. Certainly, many people *are* victims, but they don't have to *stay* victims. When people don't learn to forgive, grieve, and move ahead with their lives, they get stuck. When they think of themselves or tell their life's story, they describe themselves as "the one who was wronged." They believe that this identity gives them a free pass to feel sorry for themselves and blame anyone and everyone for every difficulty they face. Playing the role of a victim validates their anger at those who have hurt them. Resentment gives them a reason to get up in the morning and provides an adrenaline rush of energy each day. Self-pity and resentment are addictive. People who remain perpetual victims thrive on it, they crave it, and they can't seem to live without it. But it's a spiritual acid that corrodes everything beautiful in their lives.

Rahab's story is full of hope and courage. She refused to remain stuck as a hopeless, helpless victim. She saw a choice to step out of the rut her life had become, and she took it. Her mind might have raced with a hundred excuses to say "No," but she found a way to say "Yes" to God. She was a foreigner and a harlot. She had no titles to impress anyone. She was an outcast among her own people, but faith changed everything. She had been a child of hell, but she became a citizen of heaven. She'd been a shady lady, but she became a shining star. She'd been a call girl, but she was now a converted girl. She moved from a house of shame to the Hall of Fame. Her identity and destiny were transformed by the grace of God. Rahab's choices weren't just about saving her own skin. Her decision also saved the lives of those she loved. In the same way, the decisions we make today have an impact on every person in our families—in this generation and in ones to follow. We aren't islands in the river of life. The choices we make have a profound impact for good or ill on those we love. I don't say this to threaten anyone or make people feel guilty. God is the God of second chances. If He's willing to turn the page for a prostitute in Jericho, He can do it for all of us.

We can see people with God's eyes.

Have we given up on a family member? Do we walk past people who are physically or morally dirty because we don't want to touch them? Years ago, I became aware that hundreds of prostitutes worked in our community. I'd known they were there, but I had no idea there were so many, and I hadn't let the reality of their desperation sink in. When I realized their plight, it broke my heart. I told a staff member, "I want you to go down the street and hire five prostitutes for an hour. Pay them whatever they charge. Put them in the church van and bring them back here to me." She thought I'd lost my mind, but she did it. While she was gone, a table with linen, candles, china, and flowers was set. We provided a wonderful meal for them. When the prostitutes walked in, I invited them to sit at the table. My wife Elizabeth sang them a beautiful song, and we gave them each a red rose. I told them about the love of Jesus and explained that God sees them as precious, beautiful roses. The hearts of these street-hardened women melted. They cried, and several of them said, "No one has ever treated us like this. Thank you so much." They gave us back the money we'd paid them. It was the beginning of a ministry to prostitutes God has used to change many lives.

We walk by wounded, ashamed, hopeless people every day. We may be able to identify many of them easily by their clothes, their smell, or the way they talk, but others look perfectly respectable and hide their desperation so no one will know they feel like the scum of the earth. They work next to us, live down the street from us, sit next to us in church, and maybe even live in our homes. They may not be walking the streets in short skirts, but they've prostituted themselves to success, drugs, popularity, wealth, comfort, or power. They live in a web of deception as strong as Rahab's.

> Will we have eyes to notice the Rahabs around us? If we notice, do we care? If we open our hearts to them, amazing things can happen.

Will we have eyes to notice the Rahabs around us? If we notice, do we care? If we open our hearts to them, amazing things can happen. Not everyone will respond with open hearts and gratitude. Most of them are so hurt they need to be convinced we don't have an angle. They've created a powerful shield to protect themselves from hurt, but the barrier also keeps them from trusting people who love them. Sooner or later, a steady drip of God's love and our kindness will make a difference, and hearts will be transformed.

Compassion costs us.

Compassion is good, right, and noble. We have to realize, though, that caring for people always has a price tag. Stopping to mend broken hearts and shattered lives requires an investment of time and other resources. Many individuals and churches don't want to pour themselves into people who are "unclean" and take so long to see substantial progress, even when they respond to the gospel. People today want instant success, and ministries of compassion rarely meet this standard.

There's another risk when we step into the lives of the down-and-out: potential damage to our reputations. I've been criticized by leaders of some churches who believed we'd "lost our calling" by giving so much attention to prostitutes, addicts, single moms, and other disenfranchised people.

The Christian faith isn't about getting; it's about giving. Far too many Christians don't understand this basic principle of spiritual life, so they have empty, impoverished hearts. Jesus told His disciples (including us),

> "Whoever wants to be my disciple must deny themselves and take up their cross and follow me. For whoever wants to save their life will lose it, but whoever loses their life for me will find it. What good will it be for someone to gain the whole world, yet forfeit their soul? Or what can anyone give in exchange for their soul?" (Matthew 16:24-26)

We gain by giving, we rise by bowing to serve, and we're filled by pouring ourselves out to God and others. This isn't a new concept. The paradox has been central to the faith since time began, and we have a supreme example. Saint Augustine captured the paradoxical wonder of Christ when he wrote:

"Man's maker was made man that He, Ruler of the stars, might nurse at His mother's breast; that the Bread might hunger, the Fountain thirst, the Light sleep, the Way be tired on his journey; that the Truth might be accused of false witness, the Teacher be beaten with whips, the Foundation be suspended on wood; that Strength might grow weak; that the Healer might be wounded; that Life might die."[3]

Christians talk about "becoming like Christ." Augustine captured what the phrase really means. True transformation happens when powerful people become humble and timid people become bold.

It's not enough to have a hit-and-run message of grace to people who are deeply hurt and have lost hope. We need staying power. We have to hang in there with a prodigal child, a friend who is an addict, someone who is chronically sick, or anyone else who requires extra grace.

After starting with the dinner for the five prostitutes, our church created a place for prostitutes to flourish. It's called the Chicago Dream Center. One of the most important human qualities is the ability to dream. For outcasts and those who have suffered from chronic failure, the ability to dream has been shattered. We wanted to create a place where dreams could be rekindled, but we don't expect instant results. These women have to rebuild every belief, value, and relationship in their lives, which takes time and effort. Our program has three stages that last two years. At this point, 300 women have successfully completed the program. (I'll explain more about this program in a later chapter.) They've regained their sanity, gotten free of drugs, found their

---

3   Augustine, *Sermons* 191.1

identity in their relationship with Christ, learned to trust again, been reunited with their kids and parents, and gained skills for successful employment.

Marisol is one of those women.

A NEW PAGE . . . A NEW BOOK

We invited Marisol to leave the streets and come to the Chicago Dream Center. She had many unanswered questions, but she was desperate enough to give it a shot. She knew something had to change or she was going to die. Marisol weighed only 82 pounds. She detoxed for a few days in the hospital. When she got out, she came to church in short shorts. She thought she looked hot. Our church has a residential discipleship facility about three hours from Chicago. We call it "the farm." We asked the ladies who were going to the farm to come to the altar for prayer, and Marisol came up. We asked God to work a miracle of transformation.

We asked God to work a miracle of transformation.

For the next two years, Marisol lived with other women rebuilding their lives. As her mind cleared, she could hear and understand the message of the gospel, and she trusted in Christ. Drugs and sex had devastated her body, but gradually her health improved. She looked like a person again! In Bible studies, classes, and countless conversations, she began to develop a new way of thinking, and she found a powerful sense of hope. She fell in love with God and His Word. By the end of her time in the Chicago Dream Center, I asked, "What is your dream now? What are you going to do with your life?"

She wasn't sure what the future held, but I had an idea. I told her, "Marisol, I'd like for you to run our café. Would you be willing to do that?"

She was thrilled. Buried underneath her addiction to drugs and prostitution was a woman with outstanding management and leadership skills. She's doing a fantastic job as the director of our Café. She plays a powerful role of loving, discipling, and coaching women who are participating in the Chicago Dream Center. She's having a profound impact on them.

As Marisol's life began to change, she wanted to reconnect with the three children she had abandoned. It's been a glorious reunion, and she now has custody of them. Today, Marisol's life is far different from the emaciated, hopeless person I met a few years ago. God restored her. She married a godly man and added a baby girl to her lineage. God's grace works miracles—occasionally quickly, but more often over time as people respond to Him with courage and faith to face each day's challenges. Today many people are looking for signs and wonders. I see astounding miracles every day in the eyes of the women who have graduated from the Chicago Dream Center. Their new lives of faith, hope, and purpose are wonders to anyone who knew them before and can see them today.

Rahab and Marisol began with nothing, but they became heroes in God's family. If you've given up on yourself, take heart. No one is beyond the grace of God. He still changes lives. If you love someone who is far from God, don't give up. Keep loving, keep giving, and keep speaking the truth. Someday, maybe the one you love will take Christ's hand. The past, no matter how evil and twisted, doesn't necessarily determine a person's future. But don't get confused—only life-changing faith in God will alter the trajectory of a person's life. Nature forms us, sin deforms us, the world conforms us, education informs us, but faith in God's love and power transforms us. If we'll give God our present, He'll redeem our future.

Some people may come to our church and turn their noses up at the volunteers with tattoos. They might wonder, *What are people like this doing in church?* They're here because they live in our community. We reached out to them on their turf, and they answered God's call to know Him and love Him. Some of the leaders of our church are former prostitutes, gangbangers, pimps, homosexuals, adulterers, and drug addicts. Some have spent a long time in prison, and some have been homeless. All of them, though, have found the love and life Christ offers, and they have become lights in their world. Today the radical transformation of their lives is the loudest and clearest testimony of the grace of God I've ever seen.

These men and women are well aware of the depth of their sins, so they are incredibly grateful for God's forgiving grace. They've lived without hope, but now they're beacons of hope to those around them. They used to take from people, but now they're thrilled to give to those in need. These people don't play "the game of church" and wear masks to impress people. They've left deception behind. They live real lives with real faith in a real God. We welcome people as different as Rahab and the Pharisee Nicodemus, wealthy Zacchaeus and the Legion-filled demoniac, rough Peter and the proper priests. Everyone has a chair at Christ's table. All are invited to come and eat. When I look at our crowd on Sunday morning, I see men and women who were shattered, empty, and angry before they met Christ. Things are different for them now— very different.

You can be sure that there are Rahabs and Marisols all around you. Don't look down on them; Jesus Christ died to show His love for them. Don't walk past them; they desperately need someone to be Christ's hands, feet, and voice in their lives. People with broken hearts and hard shells often appear to be the most unlikely sources of powerful faith, but they can become bright lights of God's grace to all around them. First, we need to show grace to them.

Are you willing to take the risk and pay the price?

CONSIDER THIS...

1. What are some ways people prostitute themselves in your community? What do they hope to gain? What do they actually lose?

2. Why do wounded people create a shell around them? What do the shells look like, sound like, and feel like? How does a shell protect them? How does it prevent them from experiencing real love?

3. Read Matthew 16:24-26. What are some of the costs of giving ourselves away? What do we gain?

4. What does the story of God's grace to Rahab say to you about
    God's hope for you?

5. Who is one person in your life who needs God's touch of grace?
    What will you do to communicate it tenderly, powerfully, and
    consistently?

2 From a Distance

For those with faith, no explanation is necessary.
For those without, no explanation is possible.
—Thomas Aquinas

Homeless women feel terribly vulnerable. They're often the victims of ruthless sexual assaults and robberies.

Doris was a woman in our neighborhood who had become homeless due to drug addiction, causing her to lose her husband, children, and career. She lived out of her car and felt secure when she parked it right under the light of our church sign. Every evening she would circle around until a parking spot opened up in front of our church. The little money she made during the day came from using her car to help people move. During one of those moves, she crossed paths with another homeless woman who told her about a new rehabilitation program she and three other women were chosen to participate in. Doris knew nothing about this program, yet she was strangely interested and continued to think about it from time to time.

One day when she was away, Doris' car was towed, leaving her with nowhere to turn. That night she went to a nearby park to sleep on a bench, where she met a man from our church who was part of a group reaching out to the homeless with food. As he shared his testimony, Doris didn't realize he represented the same church whose light had provided protection for her. Later, when she met our people face to face, she began to discover the heart behind the light.

Throughout the day, people had kept telling Doris that a lady was looking for her. Being a woman living on the streets, she wasn't sure she wanted the lady to find her. After she went to sleep on the bench that night, she was awakened by the same woman who had told her about that new program a while back. One of the ladies had dropped out of the program and there was an open spot. Doris decided to jump at the opportunity.

Doris took a leap of faith when she decided to enter the Chicago Dream Center's rehabilitation program. Even though she didn't know much about Jesus, she decided to put her trust in Him to bring healing and transformation to her life.

A DESPERATE OFFICER

Some of us make excuses for our lack of faith: we've only been Christians for a short time, we've experienced some major setbacks in our lives, or we aren't highly educated in biblical truth. One time Jesus was amazed at the faith of a man who had no spiritual assets, yet offered no excuses. He was a foreigner, a Roman centurion who had been worshiping Caesar as his god. However, the officer understood something very important about Jesus—His supreme authority. Even though his spiritual background gave him very few clues about Christ, he believed Jesus could perform miracles, even at a distance.

Every person is born with an innate if undefined belief system. We may have grown up hearing the best Bible teacher in the world, or we may have lived in the backside of nowhere, but God has put a sense of

His presence and power in the heart of every person on earth. In his letter to the Romans, Paul explained, "What may be known about God is plain to them, because God has made it plain to them. For since the creation of the world God's invisible qualities—his eternal power and divine nature—have been clearly seen, being understood from what has been made, so that people are without excuse" (Romans 1:19-20).

The centurion was a pagan who served Caesar. His faith was misplaced; it needed to be redirected. He also had a deep and profound grasp of the power of authority. In the military, rank rules. He was in charge of 100 soldiers, and he knew that orders must be followed. Today, our young people may resist the authority of their parents, teachers, and other leaders, but the centurion didn't have this problem. Still, he wasn't a hardened man. He valued authority because he knew it could be used to care for people as well as oppress them.

For months the centurion had heard stories about a man who was traveling around Galilee preaching strange new truths and healing people. The incredible news about Jesus had spread throughout the entire province. Even without modern telecommunications, rumors of a man who healed the sick, raised the dead, cleansed lepers, and cast out demons had spread like wildfire! Some people thought this stranger was a prophet; others believed He was crazy. As long as He didn't cause any trouble in the centurion's city, he didn't pay much attention—until he realized how much he needed Him.

Luke tells us the centurion had a servant who was sick and dying. The officer loved his servant. His affection is remarkable because the servant was probably a Jew. Every part of this story turns things upside down. The Jews typically despised the Roman occupiers—especially the officers who brutally oppressed them. But this centurion loved his servant, and his love was so obvious that he won the respect of the Jewish elders in the city. Love had turned bitterness into loyalty.

The centurion sent the elders to ask Jesus to heal his sick servant. When they met Him, they didn't just make a request. They pleaded, "This man deserves to have you do this, because he loves our nation and has built our synagogue" (Luke 7:4-5).

Jesus agreed to go with them to the centurion's home. On the way, one of the most remarkable events in the Gospels occurred. Luke wrote,

[Jesus] was not far from the house when the centurion sent friends to say to him: "Lord, don't trouble yourself, for I do not deserve to have you come under my roof. That is why I did not even consider myself worthy to come to you. But say the word, and my servant will be healed. For I myself am a man under authority, with soldiers under me. I tell this one, 'Go,' and he goes; and that one, 'Come,' and he comes. I say to my servant, 'Do this,' and he does it" (Luke 7:6-8).

The Roman officer wasn't full of himself. He didn't demand to be coddled or entertained by Jesus. He wasn't looking for affirmation or validation. He was so humble that he didn't think he was worthy of Jesus' effort to come to his house. His humility, though, wasn't the kind that says, "Look at me. I'm so pitiful." It was the kind that says, "I'm not important, but You are supremely important. I trust You to accomplish Your purposes because of Your character, power, and love—not mine."

Jesus had been spending time with Jewish leaders and common people in every city where He traveled. They hadn't just *heard* stories about His love and power. They'd *seen* it with their own eyes! In every town, however, many people were skeptical. Even around His own campfires each night, His closest followers couldn't quite believe He was Jehovah in the flesh. But here was a Roman officer with remarkable faith. As a foreigner, he wouldn't be allowed to enter the inner courts of the temple in Jerusalem, but his faith dwarfed that of the Jews.

Jesus was blown away. He "marveled" at the centurion's trust. He told the people on the road that day, "I tell you, I have not found such great faith even in Israel" (Luke 7:9). In other words, "How can this happen? My own people have the Scriptures, but they don't believe very well. My own people have seen Me heal the sick, cast out demons, and restore sight to the blind, but they're still suspicious of Me. Yet this man trusts Me so much that he doesn't even need to see Me to believe. I'm shocked. This man has great faith!" When the men returned to the centurion's house, they found the servant completely healed.

What did the centurion believe? He may not have understood that Jesus was the Messiah foretold by the ancient Jewish prophets, but he certainly grasped the fact that He had the power to heal his servant, even at a distance. His knowledge was incomplete, but his faith was strong in what he knew.

I can imagine the looks on the disciples' faces as the conversation unfolded. They were the chosen ones, the inner circle, the ones who had been handpicked by Jesus to follow Him and represent Him. But when Jesus said, "I haven't seen faith like this in Israel," He meant them, too—and they knew it. I believe Jesus was using the centurion's grasp of His authority to throw down a challenge. He was implicitly telling His disciples, "Okay, you're on. If a Roman officer can trust Me like this, where's your faith? You need to see My authority to believe, but he only needed to hear about Me. You have to be in My presence, and you believe poorly. He doesn't even need to meet Me! You don't understand My authority, but he gets it."

Jesus is throwing down the same challenge to you and me.

DO WE BELIEVE?

The centurion's faith amazed Jesus. How can we develop this kind of vibrant trust in God?

Look up, look down.

Like the centurion, we may not have all the information in the world about Jesus, but that doesn't excuse us from trusting Him to do incredible things. If we wait until we know it all, we'll never take a step of faith. God has given us the ability to recognize the marvel of creation, which clearly demonstrates the ultimate authority of God. Telescopes and microscopes can be instruments of worship. We just need to walk outside and open our eyes to see the incredible expanse of the heavens. They shout that God is powerful, creative, and trustworthy! Or we can look through a microscope to see the details in cells and the structure of DNA. Nothing is too small to escape God's care and control. Yes, we need the specific revelation of the Bible to know more of the character and purposes of God, but general revelation in nature is a pretty big book! We have enough to trust Him.

If the thrill is gone in your relationship with Christ, let the stars speak to your heart. Ptolemy, the first astronomer, looked at the night sky and counted 1056 stars. With the magnification of a one-inch telescope, we can see 225,000 stars; with a 100-inch telescope, we can see 1.5 billion stars; and with a 200-inch telescope, we can see 1 billion galaxies, each with about 200 billion stars. The Hubble telescope can see 200 billion galaxies. Such numbers quickly become meaningless, so one astronomer put it this way: 100 billion stars in each of 100 billion galaxies represent the grains of sand on every shore on every beach throughout the entire world! And each of those grains of sand represents an object millions of times larger than our earth.

To measure great distances, astronomers use units called *light-years*: the distance light travels in a year. At 186,000 miles per second, light travels about six trillion miles in a year. Light from our sun takes more than eight minutes to reach the earth, and about seven hours to reach Pluto. The next nearest star in our galaxy is Alpha Centauri, which is 4.3 light-years away. In other words, the light astronomers see from Alpha Centauri today left there over four years ago.

How do we respond to the incredible facts of the universe? With wide-eyed wonder at the magnificence of the creation and the God who spoke and created it all. The psalmist exclaimed,

> Many, LORD my God,
>> are the wonders you have done,
>> the things you planned for us.
> None can compare with you;
>> were I to speak and tell of your deeds,
>> they would be too many to declare (Psalm 40:5).

In *Astronomy*, Dr. Arthur Harding wrote, "Who can study the science of astronomy and contemplate the star-lit heavens with a knowledge of the celestial bodies, their movements and their enormous distances, without bowing his head in reverence to the power that brought this universe into being and safely guides its individual members?"[4]

Every molecule in the universe obeys God's authority. The winds are under His control, and He knows what's happening every second on

---

4   Dr. Arthur Harding, *Astronomy* (Doubleday & Co.: New York, 1977), cited in *God Attachment*, Tim Clinton and Josh Straub, 200.

the farthest star 13.7 billion light-years away from us. Can He heal a sick servant from a distance? No sweat. Can He take care of the problems in your life and mine. A piece of cake.

Take a bold step to care for others.

The centurion's understanding of Christ's authority wasn't a nice fact he left on a shelf. He based his life—and the life of his servant—on this truth. He was willing to expose himself to ridicule from his fellow soldiers by publicly putting his faith in Jesus. James famously wrote that "faith without works is dead" (James 2:17). The centurion's faith brought life.

> He loved his Jewish servant so much that he risked his reputation to ask an itinerant preacher to heal him.

In the Roman world, citizens and soldiers looked down on people in the conquered provinces. The centurion, however, refused to be a bully. He loved his Jewish servant so much that he risked his reputation to ask an itinerant preacher to heal him. He could have let this servant die. After all, there were plenty of others who could take his place—but he loved his servant. To the officer, the servant wasn't just a man who performed tasks to make his life easier. He was a flesh and blood person of value.

The centurion probably didn't know it, but his care for his servant was consistent with the teaching of the ancient prophets—and consistent with the life of Jesus, too. Caring for foreigners and outcasts has always been important to God. The Jews somehow missed that. Over the years, they embraced the teaching that they were God's favored nation, but they overlooked the part about God using them to bless every nation on earth.

Many of us miss it, too. Why are we oblivious to our privilege and responsibility to care for those around us? Because we don't understand God's heart.

One time a man asked Jesus to identify the most important of the 613 commandments. He said it's to "love God with all our hearts" and "love people like we love ourselves" (Matthew 22:36-39). What would that look like? It means God's love gives us more delight than anything in the world, and we try to meet the needs of others with the same level of intensity and devotion with which we address our own. Like the man who heard Jesus' answer, we find this an extreme challenge, and we look for an out. But there's not one. Loving God and people—all people— with our whole hearts is His design for us.

Jesus' teaching about the supreme priority of loving God and loving people isn't isolated to this one passage. It's found throughout the Scriptures. For instance, when Micah described what's most important to God, he wrote,

> He has shown you, O mortal, what is good.
> And what does the LORD require of you?
> To act justly and to love mercy
> and to walk humbly with your God (Micah 6:8).

Justice and mercy aren't two different concepts. Justice isn't just punishment of wrongs; it's also protection of the vulnerable and care for the needy. Justice and mercy go hand in hand. To make it crystal clear, Zechariah recorded God's personal instructions about often overlooked groups of people:

> This is what the LORD Almighty said: "Administer true justice; show mercy and compassion to one another. Do not oppress the widow or the fatherless, the foreigner or the poor. Do not plot evil against each other" (Zechariah 7:9-10).

In his book, *Generous Justice,* pastor and author Tim Keller comments on this passage: "In premodern, agrarian societies, these four groups had no social power. They lived at subsistence level and were only days from starvation if there was any famine, invasion, or even minor social unrest. Today this quartet would be expanded to include the refugee, the migrant worker, the homeless, and many single parents and elderly people."[5]

According to the Bible, it's serious business to neglect the people God loves. Moses told the people, "Cursed is anyone who withholds justice from the foreigner, the fatherless or the widow." Then all the people shall say, "Amen!" (Deuteronomy 27:19) Centuries later, Jeremiah affirmed this instruction:

> This is what the LORD says: Do what is just and right. Rescue from the hand of the oppressor the one who has been robbed. Do no wrong or violence to the foreigner, the fatherless or the widow, and do not shed innocent blood in this place (Jeremiah 22:3).

Hundreds of years after Jeremiah, another prophet spoke about the necessity of having active compassion to care for those in need. Jesus said that a sure mark of a saved heart is love for the hurting:

> "Then the King will say to those on his right, 'Come, you who are blessed by my Father; take your inheritance, the kingdom prepared for you since the creation of the world. For I was hungry and you gave me something to eat, I was thirsty and you gave me something to drink, I was a stranger and you invited

5   Tim Keller, *Generous Justice* (Dutton: New York, 2010), 4.

me in, I needed clothes and you clothed me, I was sick and you looked after me, I was in prison and you came to visit me' " (Matthew 25:34-36).

When those listening didn't understand, the king explained, "Truly I tell you, whatever you did for one of the least of these brothers and sisters of mine, you did for me" (verse 40).

When the scribe asked Jesus about the Greatest Commandment and wasn't pleased with His answer, he tried to escape responsibility by defining his "neighbor" very narrowly. People are doing the same thing today. In our world, we sometimes hear people making a distinction between "the deserving poor" and "the undeserving poor." In their opinion, the ones who deserve care are innocent victims who suffer because of difficult circumstances: tornadoes, hurricanes, fires, or drunk drivers. It's easy to see that we should help them.

The other group of poverty victims is a bigger problem for many people. It includes addicts, alcoholics, the chronically unemployed, the homeless, and people with mental illness. Critics look down on them and sneer, "If they had made better choices, they wouldn't be in this predicament," or "They're hopeless. What's the use?" It's interesting that Jesus' description of the actions of a merciful, compassionate person in Matthew's Gospel doesn't make any distinctions about why people are hungry, thirsty, abandoned, naked, sick, or in prison. It doesn't say we should only visit prisoners who

> It's interesting that Jesus' description of the actions of a merciful, compassionate person in Matthew's Gospel doesn't make any distinctions about why people are hungry, thirsty, abandoned, naked, sick, or in prison.

are wrongly convicted or victims of political oppression. We are to visit murderers or thieves, too.

I'm afraid many people today don't have enough faith to move them to care for those around them. For the vast majority, the problem isn't information. They've heard countless stories of changed lives, but it has become background noise instead of a source of inspiration. The problem isn't access to truth. They can go to any church in their area and download messages and articles from the leading pastors and teachers. Their hearts, though, haven't been melted by the grace of God, and His supreme authority doesn't amaze them.

Supreme power is most clearly demonstrated in kindness and humility.

Christ's authority was shown in the cross. There, He gave up everything so we could know true riches. He was abandoned so we could be accepted into His family. He suffered so we can be healed. He died to give us life. Christ's act of ultimate humility demonstrated His authority to the spiritual forces in the eternal world. Paul explained, "And having disarmed the powers and authorities [the horde of demonic forces], he made a public spectacle of them, triumphing over them by the cross" (Colossians 2:15).

As Jesus suffered on the cross, a centurion noticed how He related to His accusers, His mother, and the two men crucified next to Him. Even when He was tortured and mocked, Jesus continued to pour out His love to others. At the moment of Jesus' last breath, the officer pronounced, "Surely this was a righteous man" (Luke 23:47). Could this have been the same soldier who trusted Him at a distance and now saw His face? If it was, he finally realized Jesus was the Son of God.

Authority and compassion aren't polar opposites. In God, they are inextricably intertwined, and in His people, they always go together.

Why are we so selfish and uncaring? At least part of the reason is that we're so wrapped up in our own desires and goals that we don't have time for God or others. When we are amazed at the majesty, power, and authority of Almighty God, our hearts soften and become easily molded. How does God want to mold them? He wants to make us more like Him: moved with compassion when we see the needs of those around us.

We're thoroughly human, and we're desperately needy. Power, possessions, prestige, and approval promise to fulfill us, but they can't. Only the loving authority of God can fill the hole in our hearts and overflow into the lives of those we meet each day.

Years ago, Bob Pierce visited an island off the coast of Korea to see the condition of hurting children. His heart was touched by their need. That day he wrote in the margin of his Bible, "Let my heart be broken with the things that break the heart of God." He began a ministry called Samaritan's Purse to care for needy people around the world.

What breaks your heart and mine? Do we feel anguish primarily when we don't get something we're sure we deserve, or do we weep when we see the pain in broken lives—next door or on the other side of the world?

We can be people of influence.

The centurion's respect for Christ's authority is mirrored in the respect the church can win in our culture—if we earn it by our courage and compassion. People are looking for role models to follow, and we can be the people they admire and emulate. We abdicate our position of authority if we are cowards or oppressive, but we win it when we care enough to step into people's lives, get dirty by caring for them, and love them with everything we've got.

Through a program called Hope Fest, our church has invested tens of thousands of dollars and adopted 15 schools in our community. Every August before school starts, we give all the children in the district a book bag. Our active involvement has earned the respect of school officials. I can call a lunch meeting to talk about solving a problem, and all 15 principals will show up ready to roll up their sleeves and join us in the effort to find a solution. After every election, I meet the mayor, aldermen, and the congressman from our district. We don't take a political stance at our church. I don't tell people how to vote, but we talk openly about the issues of social justice and mobilize our people to make a difference. I don't represent the donkey or the elephant. I represent the Lion.

I flew to another part of the country to meet with a pastor who asked for my help. His church wasn't growing, and he wanted my advice about how to jumpstart his attendance. As he drove me to his church, we passed the local high school. I asked, "Do you know the principal of this school?"

He responded, "No, I haven't met him."

"How long has he been the principal?" I asked.

The pastor answered, "This is his fifth year."

I probed, "Do you know your city council member?"

"No, not really."

"How about the mayor? Do you know him?"

"No."

I told him, "Brother, you will surely die."

Two years later, attendance at his church fell to almost zero, and they closed the doors. God had given the pastor spiritual authority in his community, but he hadn't used it to connect with leaders, provide services for the people, and stand up for Christ so that everyone would see the light of the gospel in his church.

Poor and marginalized people in every community need someone to stand up for them. The church is "the tip of the spear" in the fight against injustice. We need to penetrate the political structure and create enough discomfort so community leaders are willing to change. Of course, we begin with sugar, but if necessary, we deliver stronger medicine on the spear point.

Fathers have an important role of authority in their families. Wives and kids look to them for strength, wisdom and love, but many dads today are absent physically or emotionally. Being a father is one of the most demanding roles in our society, but it's also one of the most essential. Many men didn't have good role models, so they don't know what it means to be a great dad for their kids. But there are no excuses. God has given every father the privilege and responsibility of shaping their children's lives. The payoff—for good or bad—is clear. Fathers who invest time and love in their kids usually reap a lifetime of wonderful relationships with them. Those who don't invest in their children often find their kids in jail, in the hospital, or in the morgue.

A father's authority isn't exercised only when the kid is misbehaving. Dads who only blast their kids produce angry teenagers and young adults. Authority is equal parts affection and direction, especially when the child has failed in some way. Being a good father takes tenacity. We have to be consistent in our presence, attention, and involvement—not perfect, but consistent.

Men can find dozens of excuses for abdicating their responsibilities as husbands and fathers, but none of them hold water. I didn't have a dad when I was a kid, but I learned how to be involved with my three children. My dad wasn't there, but I make sure I'm there for them. Whatever it takes, I'm committed to be the father God wants me to be. When Adam and Eve sinned, God called for Adam to give an account of his actions. He was the leader of his home, not Eve. It hasn't changed since then.

Every ministry leader, teacher, and volunteer has authority to serve only because he or she has exercised appropriate authority in the home. Paul makes this very clear in his qualifications for deacons and elders (1 Timothy 3:4-5). If we shepherd our families with integrity and love, we're qualified to shepherd God's family. The quality of our relationships at home is the platform for our roles as leaders and servants in the church.

DO OVER

In her months in the Chicago Dream Center, Doris began to be amazed at the authority and kindness of God—and it changed her. She found stability, wisdom, and hope, and her joy overflowed into the lives of others. When she completed a four-month course, we saw something special in her. She was a leader who had won the respect and love of everyone around her. She stayed at the Chicago Dream Center as an intern volunteer for a year. Five years later, we anointed her to become one of the pastors for this ministry. In Doris's role as a pastor, the cycle is complete. She's a role model, mentor, and friend to the women who are trusting God to put their lives back together. Her children had seen her lost, afraid, and alone, but now they see her as a loving and lovely person God is using to touch the lives of hurting women.

Jesus was amazed by the centurion's faith in His authority. I think He's equally impressed with Doris and every other believer who takes Him at His word and trusts in His power and compassion. Authority and love are found in Jesus, and they're found in those who truly trust Him.

CONSIDER THIS...

1. What are some authorities people respect today? How do they earn our trust? What are some ways we show our respect?

2. What gave the centurion confidence in Jesus' authority? How is his faith similar or different from most people's trust in Christ?

3. What was the connection between authority and compassion in the centurion's life? What's the connection in your life?

4. Does Bob Pierce's prayer, "Let my heart be broken with the things that break the heart of God," inspire you or threaten you? Explain your answer.

5. What sciences, stories, or truths magnify God's authority in your mind and heart? What happens to you when you read and hear them?

3   Stand Up, Stand Tall

Action springs not from thought, but from a readiness for responsibility.

—Dietrich Bonhoeffer

After I became a Christian as a boy of 14, I quickly realized that being isolated in my community made me vulnerable. Everybody was connected to a group: a gang, a team, or a family of some kind. The group was the source of the members' identity and strength. With it, you had a chance to face the inevitable and almost daily attacks; without it, you had no chance at all.

Some kids face threats such as the possibility of not being asked to sit at the cool kids' lunch table or getting turned down for a date to the prom. Not in my neighborhood. Our threats were a matter of life or death. Any day I might step outside and run into gangs that used their weapons on other people, and I could be next.

When I was about 17 years old, I was walking after midnight with three younger friends down Armitage Avenue in Humboldt Park. We were going to our family's little apartment. One of my friends was riding a bike, and at one point he rode ahead of us down the street. A few minutes later, he hurried back. He stopped next to me, and with eyes wide with fear he said, "There are about 20 guys up there on the corner! What do you want us to do?"

I could read his mind. I glared at him, "What do you mean? We're not going to run."

He got off his bike and slid it under a car. We didn't want them to steal the bike, and we didn't want them to use it as a weapon if we got into a fight. The four of us kept walking. Running wasn't an option. It would have sent a message to the young thugs that we were weak, or that they were right about us being inferior, or that we were trying to hide something from them—maybe something they wanted.

As we approached them, they split up. About half of them crossed the street. They were surrounding us. Without missing a step, I walked straight to the leader. I'd never seen these young men before, but I could easily identify the leader because the others obviously deferred to him. I led the other three up to him, and I asked, "What you be about?"

He sneered, "We're the Vice Lords." He looked me up and down, and then he asked, "What you be about?"

I said, "Jesus Christ." I reached out my hand, and he took it. We shook, and then we shook hands with the other guys who were now all around us. After we'd shaken the last one, we nodded to them and continued our walk down the street. Later, we went back to get the bike.

On another occasion, some friends and I hung around talking at the church after services on a Sunday night. When we came out, a gang from another part of Chicago confronted us as we walked down the front steps. They'd come to Humboldt Park looking for some action. They probably thought it would be fun to beat up some kids who were coming out of church. When we stepped out, they quickly encircled us. They were carrying tire tools, bats, and chains. I'd never seen them before.

One of them asked, "Hey, what you be about?"

"Jesus Christ," I said boldly.

That's just what they wanted to hear. They assumed Christians would be easy prey. A couple of them took menacing steps toward us. I held up my hand. "There's a good chance you're going to take us down, but you can be sure of this: I'm going to take two of you down with me. We're Christians, but we're not punks!"

One of them asked, "Hey, what you be about?"

"Jesus Christ," I said boldly.

One of them looked at the Bibles in our hands. I could tell what he was thinking. The books looked a little lame compared to the weapons they carried. I told them, "We may be carrying Bibles, but we know how to defend ourselves."

They realized this wasn't going to be quite as easy as they thought. They looked at each other wondering what to do. One of them turned to walk away, and the rest followed without a word. In a few seconds, my friends and I were standing alone on the steps of the church.

My high school was predominately Hispanic. There were a few African-Americans and only a handful of Caucasians. On every floor of our school, gangs had a presence. Vice Lords, Disciples, Latin Kings, and Cobras staked out territory. One day as I rode the escalator down the nine flights, I saw four Disciples beating up a Caucasian guy in a stairwell. I jumped over the railing of the escalator and stood in the middle of the gang members. I put the Caucasian kid behind me, and I told the Disciples, "If you want to hit somebody, hit me!"

They yelled, "Get out of here, man! This isn't your fight."

"It is now," I told them.

I didn't know these guys, but they knew me. I'd played football, and everybody at the school knew I stood up for Christ. They were sure I meant what I said, so they backed down. The Caucasian kid was grateful and amazed. It was a good day for him.

As a pastor, I've had many opportunities to stand up against injustice. A few years ago, I was part of a boycott in our city to protest the city's policies and inequitable hiring practices. There weren't enough Hispanic teachers, principals, and police commanders. I gathered 70 other pastors, and together we made a difference. The next month, the city hired five new Hispanic police commanders. I've always considered Mayor Richard M. Daley to be a good friend, but that didn't mean I had to stay quiet when his people weren't doing the right thing. It was time to speak up, identify injustice, and lobby for change.[6]

Today many Christians don't stand up against injustice for two primary reasons: inconvenience and the risk of ridicule. Caring for the poor, addicts, the sick, the homeless, immigrants, and every other category of needy people requires time and effort. Many Christians are happy to give a few dollars and devote an hour or two, but they aren't willing to forego their normal pleasures and comforts for very long. And they've seen what happened when others have poured out their lives to help the disadvantaged and disenfranchised—they caught flak! People told them to mind their own business, and they were criticized for helping people who should be taking care of themselves.

When I spoke out against a proposed high school for gay/lesbian youth in Chicago, I made sure I wasn't perceived as standing against homosexual people. Few issues in our culture are as explosive as this one. When I was being considered as a candidate for alderman in Chicago, I had a meeting with about 30 homosexuals in our community, and

---

6   For more on this story, see Mark Brown's article, "Latino clergy standing up to Daley," Chicago *Sun Times*, February 10, 2009.

I listened carefully to them. They wanted us to make changes to our church website. They are wounded, hurting, and alone. I shared the love of Jesus with them, but I didn't back down an inch. I wanted them to know that we may differ in our beliefs, but I care for them and respect them. Some of the people who attended the meeting became members of our church. Since the day I trusted Christ and began standing up for Him, I've been a target of potential violence and constant ridicule.

> Taking a stand makes us vulnerable, but if we claim to know Jesus Christ, His compassion for the hurting will rub off on us.

Taking a stand makes us vulnerable, but if we claim to know Jesus Christ, His compassion for the hurting will rub off on us. When His love captures us, we know we can't turn and walk away from injustice. We're determined to make a difference. Remaining quiet may make life easier for a while, but it's not the way Christ lived and died.

People have always been self-absorbed, but never more than today. Sociologists have noticed an alarming trend. Daniel Yankelovich wrote *New Rules* to describe how our culture has moved from *self-sacrifice* before and during World War II to *self-indulgence* today.[7] In addition, advertising has changed in the past generation. Years ago, ads described the qualities of the product, but in recent years, they promise that the product will make the buyer more popular, cool, and comfortable. We are unapologetically self-absorbed.

In the 1960s, segregation in the South was strangling the life out of African-American people. Martin Luther King, Jr. led strikes and

---

7   Daniel Yankelovich, *New Rules* (Random House: New York, 1981), xvi.

boycotts, but he used a new technique in stark contrast to the angry mood between the races: nonviolence. King instructed his followers to avoid lashing out even when they were beaten and abused. Their tactic completely disarmed authorities like Birmingham Police Commissioner Bull Connor. King was arrested over and over again. In his famous "Letter from Birmingham Jail," he wrote, "We will have to repent in this generation not merely for the vitriolic words and actions of the bad people, but for the appalling silence of the good people." If we insist on being comfortable, we'll never take a stand for the poor and hurting.

Years ago when I was a student at North Central Bible College in Minnesota, one of my professors asked the class to write a description of "the ideal church." I wrote, "It will have shelters for the homeless and help runaway teenagers, gangbangers, and prostitutes." The list of needs in Jesus' day was long. Even in our day of incredible affluence, the list hasn't gotten any shorter. If we open our eyes, we'll see immigrants who are underpaid and overworked, children in schools without books, inadequate housing, child abuse, abandonment, domestic violence, drugs, mental illness, and families shattered by hatred and distrust.

You don't have to come to Humboldt Park in Chicago to find injustice. You will find signs and symptoms in every urban, suburban, and rural area in our country and throughout the world. We can leave the answers to the government, but it then gets caught up in power politics. We can leave it to social agencies, but they're already overwhelmed. It's our responsibility to stand up. For the church, business as usual won't cut it. Author and professor Dallas Willard observed,

> The world can no longer be left to mere diplomats, politicians and business leaders. They have done the best they could, no doubt. But this is an age for spiritual heroes—a time for men and women to be heroic in their faith and in spiritual character

and power. The greatest danger to the Christian church today is that of pitching its message too low.[8]

We might be terrified the first time we stand up against injustice, but if we stand strong, we gain confidence and courage. The next time, it's a little easier. By the tenth time, it becomes a normal part of our character and behavior. Even more, it becomes woven into the fabric of our identity—it's who we are. Soon we develop a reputation as the people who really care for those who are down-and-out. Others look to us for leadership. We become their examples and their inspiration. We don't have to be great leaders or have terrific speaking talents. We can be as humble as Mother Teresa—with a tender heart and a steel backbone.

We might be terrified the first time we stand up against injustice, but if we stand strong, we gain confidence and courage.

STOOPING . . . STANDING

In the months after Jesus died and rose to heaven, the number of believers grew fast. God was performing miracles through the apostles, and people were amazed at the power and love of God. Growth, though, always brings its share of difficulties.

A group of Grecian Jewish widows in Jerusalem felt overlooked when the resources were handed out. Maybe they didn't speak Aramaic very well, or perhaps there was racial prejudice. Whatever the cause, they complained and won a hearing. The apostles were overworked and tired. They were trying to meet all the people's physical needs in

8   Dallas Willard, *The Spirit of the Disciplines* (HarperOne: New York, 1990), xii.

addition to their spiritual needs. They couldn't keep this up, so they appointed seven men to help with the administrative duties. One of them was Stephen, "a man full of faith and of the Holy Spirit" (Acts 6:5). One of the ways to identify the character of a person is to answer the question, "What is he or she full of?" Some people are full of work or sports or their kids or drugs. Others are full of doubt, fear, jealousy, and greed. Most people, in fact, are full of themselves, but Stephen was full of faith and the Holy Spirit.

What does it mean to be full of the Holy Spirit? We might define and describe spiritual life many different ways, but in essence, it means to be so filled with the love and power of Christ that His presence overflows from us into the lives of others. That's exactly what happened with Stephen.

After the apostles chose Stephen among the seven servants (or deacons) to care for the widows' needs, he used his role to touch people's lives. Luke tells us that Stephen "did great wonders and miraculous signs among the people" (Acts 6:8). He could have found plenty of administrative work to do, but that wasn't enough for Stephen. He saw every contact, every interaction, and every circumstance as an opportunity to mend broken lives. The hurting people around him weren't nuisances; they were God's choice people who needed the power and compassion of the Spirit.

As Stephen cared for widows and trusted God to use him to meet all kinds of needs, a group of people tried to intimidate him. They were Jews from the Synagogue of the Freedmen who had come from all points of the compass: Cyrene and Alexandria in Africa and Roman provinces in modern Turkey. Stephen was surrounded! He preached the grace of Jesus to die for our sins. They couldn't stand it, so they argued with him. When they lost the argument, they acted like a lot of losers and began to spread vicious rumors about him. They found some friends who were willing to falsely accuse Stephen of blasphemy by speaking against Moses and the authority of God.

When the religious leaders heard the rumors, they were furious. They'd probably been waiting for something—anything!—to use against the new group of Christians. The accusations against Stephen were just what they wanted to hear. They brought him into their court in the Sanhedrin, the 70 men who ruled the Jewish nation, and they listened to the witnesses. By now, the accusers had expanded their charges. The witnesses claimed, "This fellow never stops speaking against this holy place and against the law. For we have heard him say that this Jesus of Nazareth will destroy this place and change the customs Moses handed down to us" (Acts 6:13-14).

In every courtroom the defendant is allowed to respond to the indictment. After the accusers spoke, the high priest asked Stephen, "Are these charges true?" (Acts 7:1) Stephen then delivered the longest, most passionate message since the Sermon on the Mount! He gave a detailed history of Israel from Abraham to that day, and he showed how every priest, prophet, and king pointed to the ultimate priest, prophet, and king: Jesus Christ. When the Jewish leaders didn't listen to his clear and reasoned presentation of the gospel, Stephen stood tall. He knew that the hard truth was the only bullet he had left in his gun. Sometimes, the only way to tenderize a heart is to blast it with confrontational truth. He told the Jewish leaders,

"You stiff-necked people, with uncircumcised hearts and ears! You are just like your fathers: you always resist the Holy Spirit! . . . And now you have betrayed and murdered [Jesus]—you who have received the law that was put into effect through angels but have not obeyed it" (Acts 7:51-53).

When the members of the Sanhedrin heard Stephen's accusations, they were outraged! Stephen hadn't backed down before, and he certainly wasn't intimidated now. He knew the punishment for blasphemy, but before they could grab him to take him out to stone him to death, he "looked up to heaven and saw the glory of God, and Jesus standing at the right hand of God. 'Look,' he said, 'I see heaven open and the Son of Man standing at the right hand of God'" (Acts 7:55-56).

When they heard Stephen's words, the leaders went berserk! They put their hands over their ears, screamed, and jumped on Stephen. They dragged him outside and began pummeling him with rocks. The ancient world knew nothing of lethal injection to execute prisoners quickly and painlessly. When someone was stoned to death, a crowd of angry men grabbed rocks weighing several pounds each, walked up to the person, and hurled the stones at him with all their might. Some of the stones hit soft tissue and gashed holes; some broke bones. To prolong the suffering, the executioners avoided hitting the person in the head. It was a brutal, vicious way to die.

To have freedom of motion to throw stones at Stephen, the men took off their outer robes and put them at a man's feet for safekeeping. The man was Saul of Tarsus, another leader of the Jews. (We see this man again a few chapters later as Paul, who became a devout follower of Jesus.)

As the stones crushed Stephen's bones and tore his flesh, the pain must have been excruciating. Even in agony, Stephen kept his heart focused on Jesus. He prayed, "Lord Jesus, receive my spirit." In his last breath, he prayed again, "Lord, do not hold this sin against them" (Acts 7:59-60).

We can tell a lot about people by their last words. John Wesley was the founder of the Methodist movement in the eighteenth century. As he lay dying, he reached out to hold the hands of those who were with him, and he said, "The best of all is that God is with us!" He lifted his hands and said it again, "The best of all is that God is with us!" Then he died. Jonathan Edwards lived in the same era. He was known as one of the most powerful preachers in

> As the rocks pummeled Stephen's body, he didn't ask God to rain down fire to take revenge on those who were killing him. He asked God to forgive them, and then he died.

American history. As he approached death, he gave final instructions to his wife and friends. Then he anticipated stepping into the presence of God. He smiled, "Where is Jesus, my true and never failing Friend?" And he died. As the rocks pummeled Stephen's body, he didn't ask God to rain down fire to take revenge on those who were killing him. He asked God to forgive them, and then he died.

Stephen's story is one of sacrifice, but it's more than that. Why was he willing to give his life for a cause? Plenty of people have sacrificed money, time, reputation, and even their lives for a cause bigger than themselves. A compelling purpose grabs their hearts. In this case, it wasn't *a cause* that captured Stephen's heart—it was *a person*. The love, power, and majesty of Christ overwhelmed Stephen. He knew that life had no meaning apart from his relationship with Jesus, and with Him, everything in his life came into sharp focus. He gladly put every dollar, every relationship, every talent, and every resource at Christ's feet. He wanted every minute of every day to honor the One who died for him. That's what it means to be "filled with the Spirit." Some people boldly talk about their devotion to Christ during good times, but when they encounter ridicule or obstacles, they bail out. Stephen knew he faced death for his defense of the gospel, and he was willing to pay any price.

But remember: Stephen's ministry didn't begin in the courtroom with the drama of his passionate defense of Christ. He was picked to be one of the seven deacons because he had demonstrated administrative faithfulness and effectiveness. Church leaders knew they could count on him to care for widows in a crisis. Because he was faithful in small things, God gave him a big test—and he passed with flying colors.

When Jesus is described after His ascension into heaven, He is pictured seated at the Father's right hand. (See Psalm 110:1, Mark 16:19, Acts 2:33, and Revelation 3:21.) Before Stephen was stoned, however, he saw Christ "standing at the right hand of God." Why is this significant? When a highly respected person walks into a room even today, people stand. As Stephen was about to step off the earth and into heaven, Jesus was showing him great respect by standing for him. When we take a stand for Jesus, He stands up to honor us. Stephen's faith amazed Jesus, and He stood to welcome him into heaven.

Jesus told His followers, "I tell you, whoever publicly acknowledges me before others, the Son of Man will also acknowledge before the angels of God. But whoever disowns me before others will be disowned before the angels of God" (Luke 12:8-9). Stephen had publicly proclaimed Jesus. Now, Jesus showed the angels He was proud of Stephen. We have countless opportunities to "publicly acknowledge" Jesus—at Christmas parties, in office hallways, over backyard fences, in study groups, in the stands at games, in our living rooms, and everywhere else people interact. We don't have to stand up and deliver a long sermon like Stephen did, but we can look for opportunities to lovingly and boldly talk about what Jesus has done for us.

Jesus wasn't standing when the first rock was thrown, but He stood when Stephen had suffered from hundreds of blows and was about to die. Some of us give up when the first rock of criticism is thrown at us.

We feel hurt, and we say, "That's it. I'm out of here. I didn't sign up for people to ridicule me for my faith." As stone after stone hit Stephen, he didn't curse his attackers, whine that the abuse was unfair, or pick up a rock and throw it back at them. What gave him such courage? He was filled with the Holy Spirit and entrusted himself to Jesus. When we're filled with the Spirit, He'll give us love even for those who hate us, and we'll stand up tall to represent Jesus to everyone who will listen.

If we don't take a stand for something, we'll fall for anything. But if we stand up for Christ, we'd need to have open eyes and full hearts. If we're to follow Stephen's example, we need to be prepared to stand alone, to be hit with some rocks, and to speak the unvarnished truth. Our courage to stand tall will cost us, but it earns Jesus' applause—and He may use our love and courage to transform people who are watching. We usually want to avoid suffering at all costs, but we need to realize we always have an audience. If people in our homes, offices, fields, and neighborhoods see us trust God in the middle of our suffering, they will be amazed and attracted. Centuries ago when Christians were thrown to the lions, Justin Martyr said, "The blood of the martyrs is the seed of the church." That's still true today.

> If people in our homes, offices, fields, and neighborhoods see us trust God in the middle of our suffering, they will be amazed and attracted.

Even in false accusation and unjust execution, Stephen left a lasting impression. When he died, he was a seed of truth in the life of at least one of the men who collaborated in his execution. Saul was holding people's cloaks, but God was getting ready to hold Saul's heart. Saul had been in Jerusalem when Jesus had been tried, falsely accused, and executed. He'd probably heard (or at least heard reports of) Jesus on the cross praying, "Father, forgive them because they don't know what they're doing." Now he heard Stephen pray almost the same words. Both of them asked God to be merciful to those who where murdering them. Saul may have connected the dots—if not then, certainly later.

Stephen was humble and bold. As a deacon, he was willing to serve in obscurity with no acclaim and no notice of his efforts, but he used every opportunity to tell people about Christ. And when he faced fierce, life-threatening opposition, he didn't back off. This blend of humility and boldness is rare. I know plenty of people who are humble but not bold. They equate humility with weakness, and they shrink to nothing when courage is demanded. I also know men and women who are as bold as lions but lack humility. They take strong stands, but the people around them often feel trampled on. What was the source of Stephen's combination of humility and boldness? He believed the gospel—not just in a superficial, intellectual way, but so deeply that it transformed his life. The grace of Jesus Christ enabled him to be honest about his sins and flaws so he could experience the depths of God's forgiveness, and as a redeemed child of God, he realized nothing mattered but the reputation of Jesus. The grace of the gospel humbled his heart and stiffened his backbone. It can do the same for us.

COURAGE, RISK, AND REWARD

In the Christian world today, some pastors and teachers claim that if we stand up for Christ, He'll make all opposition fall in front of us. That's rarely the case. Sometimes our adversaries try to intimidate us, and if we stand up to them, they quickly fade away. But many of those who oppose us—in the spiritual and physical worlds—are strong and smart. They don't back down easily, and in fact, they redouble their opposition. We're in a war, and we expect to have casualties. Jesus suffered for doing the right and noble thing. If we follow Him, we can expect to suffer, too. In his book, *Extravagant*, pastor Brian Jarrett observes,

> Too often in the American church, we believe the doctrines of the cross, and we can explain the concepts of justification and reconciliation, but we don't grasp the implication of these truths. The cross of Christ sets us free from sin, but it calls us to devote every ounce of our lives to the One who bought our freedom. We are, as Paul explained, "no longer our own. We've been bought with a price" (1 Corinthians 6:19-20). Jesus isn't our Sunday Civic Club president, and church shouldn't be just a social gathering. The church is a combination hospital and command center, the place where hurting people receive comfort and the launching pad to conquer and transform the world! With this insight, we realize that the purpose of our lives doesn't come from having one more possession, one more promotion, or one more pleasure. It comes from knowing that our lives really count in God's kingdom.[9]

Did things turn out well for Stephen when he stood up for Christ? He was killed, so from the human perspective, it was a disaster. However, from the viewpoint of eternity, it was a glorious outcome. Out of respect, Jesus stood to welcome him home. It doesn't get any better than that! As we look at Stephen's life, we see several principles we can apply.

---

9   Brian Jarrett, *Extravagant* (Influence Resources: Springfield, Missouri, 2011), 53-54.

Stephen's life was a beautiful blend of kindness and courage.

He cared for the disadvantaged in his community. He didn't demand a role as a speaker or a title as a church leader. He served faithfully and lovingly, but he was ready when an opportunity came knocking. When he faced opposition, he didn't back down. He stood strong to defend Jesus and the truth. When he realized he was going to be falsely convicted and executed, he condemned the religious leaders in the same way Jesus had spoken of them as "a brood of vipers" and "whitewashed tombs." And like Jesus, he cared even for those who were killing him, graciously praying for them with his last breath. He spoke confidently and boldly, but without a hint of revenge. He prayed tenderly, but without ever groveling in self-pity and weakness.

When we stand up for Christ in our communities, there are no guarantees.

We might be applauded by some people for being faithful, or we might be condemned by others for being so narrow. Whenever we stand tall for Christ, we can be sure of two things: opposition and glory. Some people will misunderstand us, and we'll need to patiently explain our mission to care for prostitutes, addicts, homeless people, and other outcasts. Still, a few will think we've lost our minds, or worse, they'll claim we're just looking for applause and power. They don't understand that nobody in his right mind would invest so much energy, heart, time, and treasure for those who don't give much back. A commitment to bring justice to the downtrodden isn't a wise investment—unless we realize the reward will come in the next life. Someday we'll hear wonderful words of affirmation, but the mayor, an alderman, other pastors, or people in our churches won't speak them—and they don't come from the President. They'll be spoken by Jesus.

Ultimately, the only thing that's important is the evaluation of God.

What people say about us may sting or encourage, but their approval isn't what matters, ultimately. Someday all the praise of people will be meaningless. Only Christ's conclusion about our lives will count. On that day, I want to hear Him say to me, "Well done, Choco! You've been a good and faithful servant. Enter into My joy!" If He's standing when He says those words, I'll be deeply honored. This understanding crystallizes my thinking, shapes my values, and gives me the determination to face any obstacle because He's worth it. Christians around the world are dying for their faith more now than any time in history, but not in America. In our country, it's socially acceptable to be a believer as long as you don't stand out too much and as long as you don't make too many waves. In our land, the risk we take usually isn't dying for our faith; it's having our friends ostracize us for being "too radical."

Expose yourself to real needs.

Do you see the injustice around you? Do you see genuine evil and the opposition to God's rule on earth? If you don't see it, you need to get out more! Even in the most affluent communities—the ones in which people spend tons of money to insulate themselves from injustice, evil, and inconvenience—heartache is behind almost every door.

Many of us have become desensitized to the needs around us. We hear about a friend whose child is on drugs, and we say only, "What a shame." We find out someone has lost his job and may lose his house, and we blandly promise, "I'll pray for you," but we forget about it.

To notice others' hurts and needs makes us vulnerable, and being vulnerable feels like a weakness. But if we want to be God's people in the real world, we have to become as vulnerable as He was—and step up to care for those around us. We need to ask, "What can our church do?" If the church isn't into social justice, we need to ask, "What can my small group, class, or circle of friends do about the needs in our community?" And if no one else is willing to take a step, you can ask, "Lord, what do you want *me* to do?" I believe God has put it in the heart of every true believer to care about widows, immigrants, refugees, prostitutes, the abused, addicts, and other hurting people. It won't be easy to stand up for them, but it's necessary. It's what Jesus did, and Stephen is our example.

Each June, our community has a seven-day Puerto Rican Festival. Years ago it began as a celebration of our culture and heritage, but soon the gangs started to dominate the atmosphere of the event. To exert a positive influence on the festival, our church held a cookout in a parking lot on one of the corners on the street. During that time, I saw gang members pull four kids out of a van and begin beating them. I immediately jumped over the fence, sprinted to the van, and stopped the fight. The gang leader recognized me. He started cursing and told me, "Pastor, this has nothing to do with you! Get out of the way!"

I stood tall and told him, "This isn't going to happen on my watch!"

He tried to argue with me, but I didn't move. Within a minute, 30 men from the cookout had joined us. When he saw them, he realized he was outnumbered. He said, "Why did you call them? And how did they get here so fast?"

I told him I hadn't called them. They just showed up. The gang leader got his guys and left. I told the four kids to get in their van and leave immediately. They were happy to get out of there alive!

My older brother is an ex-gang member. When he heard about the confrontation, he came to see me and said, "Hey, you'd better be careful. Those guys have guns, and they're pretty tough. Watch your back."

I assured him I was well aware of their reputation, but I wasn't going to let them beat up some kids while I stood there and watched.

If we open our eyes when we drive down the streets of our communities, we'll see people in need. In many parts of the country that rely on immigrant laborers, Christians can stand up to provide healthcare for undocumented workers. Some communities ask doctors and dentists to donate a day's services, and they set up free clinics. They're swamped by people in need who come for help. We don't need to have an argument over how those people got to our country. We can disagree about national policy, but they're here, and they need our help. Do we hide behind our policies and refuse to meet their needs for healthcare? They also need affordable housing and schools that have ESL (English as a Second Language) programs for their kids.

The biggest raid on undocumented workers didn't take place in Texas or California. In Postville, Iowa, 900 federal officers arrested 389 people on the day after Mother's Day in 2008. A couple of days later, my congressman called me and said, "Pastor Choco, would you take a ride with me?"

I hadn't heard about the raid. I responded, "Sure. Where are we going?"

He told me about what had happened in Postville, and the next day, six of us drove five hours to the small farming community to meet with the family members of those who had been arrested. The raid devastated the Hispanic community. The previous Sunday, one church had over 200 people in attendance. The next Sunday, there were nine. A *Washington Post* article observed, "It has upended this tree-lined community, which calls itself 'Hometown to the World.' Half of the school system's 600 students were absent Tuesday, including 90 percent of Hispanic children, because their parents were arrested or in hiding."[10] Families were torn apart, and so was my heart. A nun in a small Catholic church was trying to care for those people, and I wanted to help. The next week, we drove back with a semi-truck full of diapers, food, and clothes for the families. We went back again with another load a few months later.

When I talk to pastors about immigration policy and the needs in Hispanic communities, many Caucasian pastors feel conflicted and confused. Some of them don't want to spend valuable resources on immigrants—people who may not be around very long. Those pastors smile and acknowledge what I'm saying, but I sense a lot of resistance. One pastor looked shocked as he told me, "Pastor Choco, some of these people actually want to become *members* of our church."

Obviously, he didn't think it was appropriate to join hands with those foreigners. I asked him, "Do you take their money when you collect the offering?"

"Yes," he admitted.

I tried to remain calm. I asked, "Then how can you refuse them membership in your church?"

I told him that I would be happy to have them at our church—no questions asked.

I'm happy to report that many pastors in our country have a sensitive conscience for social justice and are reaching out to all kinds of disadvantaged and overlooked people. Every leader and every believer needs to ask some probing questions: Do we focus virtually all of our attention and resources on the people who sit in our pews each Sunday? Or are we called to be God's representative to the whole

---

10   Spenser S. Hsu, "Immigration Raid Jars a Small Town," *Washington Post*, Sunday, May 18, 2008.

community—even the foreigners? What does it mean, and what does it cost, to care for those who can't give much back?

Stephen's first job was to care for the Greek widows. They were immigrants in Jerusalem, and the church

What does it mean, and what does it cost, to care for those who can't give much back?

was dedicated to care for them. Today, as people drive to their nice churches in their fine cars, they drive past hundreds or even thousands of people who are homeless, who can't speak English, who don't have a job, are mentally ill, or are desperate in some other way. Maybe some Sundays we ought to skip church and spend the hour getting out of the car to talk to the people we've passed so many times before.

It's an amazing fact of psychology that most people aren't ever satisfied with their level of income and comfort. Many years ago, John D. Rockefeller was the richest man in the world. When a reporter asked him how much money he needed to make him happy, he said, "Just a little bit more. Just a little bit more."

We need to look at the incredible wealth we enjoy and devote it all to Jesus Christ. We are His, and everything on earth is His. Two passages of Scripture inspire me. Jesus said, "From everyone who has been given much, much will be demanded; and from the one who has been entrusted with much, much more will be asked" (Luke 12:48). We've been given so much. We are the wealthiest nation the earth has ever seen. Half the world's population—over three billion people—lives on less than $2.50 a day,[11] but even those classified as "poor people" in our country have cars, cable television, clothes, and food. What are we doing with all God has given us?

11   "Poverty Facts and Stats," Anup Shah, *Global Issues*, September 10, 2010.

The second passage comes from John's first letter. He wrote, "This is how we know we are in him: Whoever claims to live in him must walk as Jesus did" (1 John 2:6). Jesus was so certain of the Father's love and power that He was completely dedicated to honor Him. He didn't think of Himself. He took retreats when He was tired, but His exhaustion didn't come from self-indulgent activities. He saw the needs of people, that they were like sheep without a shepherd, and He tended those sheep.

What do you see when you look around? What do I see?

Do you want to be like Stephen, full of humility and boldness? Develop a deep faith in Stephen's God. Let His forgiveness free you from being self-absorbed, and let His purpose drive you to stand tall to make Him famous.

STANDING TALL IN OUR COMMUNITY

Our church has grown from 68 people in 2000 to over 12,000 today because we've stood up like Stephen in our community. When those 68 unanimously asked me to be their pastor, they already knew me. I'd married the pastor's daughter, and I'd been serving in the church for several years. Immediately, I identified the needs in our community: gangs, single moms, homelessness, and addiction. The community was coming apart at the seams. We simply couldn't keep doing church in the same way if we wanted to have a dramatic impact on people. Inside the church, we renewed a commitment to excellence; outside, we got involved in schools, cleaning streets, and all kinds of outreaches to connect with people in the neighborhoods.

The possibilities to stand up against injustice are almost endless. We opened the first shelter for Hispanic homeless people on our side of Chicago. It was called The River of Life. At that time, school districts in other parts of the city were receiving funds to revive facilities and buy computers and new books, but our community was left out. We lobbied the Mayor and the CEO of Chicago Public Schools to change their priorities so our kids could receive a first-rate education. In fact, I was so committed to this effort that I became the Executive Assistant to the CEO of the Chicago Public Schools. I was an insider.

> Standing up boldly against injustice gave our church disproportionate influence in the community.

Standing up boldly against injustice gave our church disproportionate influence in the community. In the early stages, we didn't have a lot of money to throw at problems. We only had a voice, but we spoke loudly, clearly, and often so we would get the attention of city officials. Soon people who benefited from our efforts started showing up at our services on Sundays. They said, "Because you help my child and care for the disadvantaged, I want to find out what you're all about." We told them about Jesus.

We mobilized our people to rub shoulders with residents on every street in our community. In the summer, we drove a truck around to give ice cream to children. We sent an army of workers into the neighborhoods to clean up the streets and put trash in dumpsters. We had cookouts, participated in parades, removed snow from driveways, fed 150 families through Manna for Life, and we began Gangs to Grace to help gangbangers get out of their destructive lifestyles and find new hope in Christ. Over the years, people realized we're not just playing church. We're creating a movement that's making a difference, and a lot of people want to join a movement of love and justice. We grew so large that we had to plant other churches with the same DNA so more people could join us.

One day in 2003, the Police Commissioner came to see me. She told me her officers had arrested 600 prostitutes in our area in the previous nine months. She asked, "Reverend, what are you going to do about this problem?"

I was surprised, and I answered honestly, "I have no idea, but I'll pray about it."

After she left, I began praying, and the Lord put the word "farm" on my heart. I had no clue what it meant. The next Sunday, I announced, "I don't know what this means, but someone here has a farm, and God wants you to give it up."

No one came forward. I wasn't sure if I was being obedient or crazy. For the next nine months, I made the same announcement. Finally, a lady came up to tell me that her uncle's wife had died. The couple had a 150-acre farm three hours from Chicago, and her uncle wanted to sell it to the church. The farm became an integral part of our strategy to rescue and restore prostitutes.

First, our people go out to the streets on Friday nights to invite the women to come to the Chicago Dream Center. Those who come stay there for three months. During that time, they detox to get off drugs, and they begin the process of emotional, relational, and spiritual healing. The women then go to the farm for eight to twelve months for concentrated work to rebuild their minds, recondition their values, and restore their hearts. Our staff members teach them God's Word and pray with them. They come back to our neighborhood with new hope and a vision for their future. We assist them in finding an apartment and a job, and we help them reconnect with their children and parents. I've had a front row seat to watch God radically transform more than 200 women.

Our commitment to justice took an upward turn a few summers ago when gang violence shattered the relative calm of Humboldt Park. I led a march for peace, called "Exodus 20:13," and we camped out in the park in our community. We invited pastors and civic leaders to join us in a show of solidarity. After we marched, many of us pitched a prayer tent that night, including my wife Elizabeth and our three children. We wanted to show there was nothing to fear.

The march at Humboldt Park was so successful that pastors in other parts of the city asked us to join them in marches there. Several of us from the Hispanic area of the city joined hands with African-American pastors and parishioners to march for peace and justice in their neighborhoods. The Mayor of Chicago joined us for the marches.

We began in our neighborhood, moved to help people throughout our city and our state, and recently, God has led us to have an even wider impact. We became aware that the high school dropout rate among Hispanics in Camden, New Jersey, was 70 percent. I brought government officials from Washington, D.C. to meet with the Mayor and school officials in the city to address this problem. Changes are happening slowly, but they're happening.

Do you have a heart to help one group of disadvantaged people? Can you mobilize a few people who will join you?

Some people might read about what our church is doing and shrug, "Well, that's great, but we don't have the resources to do all that." We didn't either when we started. The only resource we had was a deep compassion for hurting people. That's all. If you have that, you can make a difference.

Do you have a heart to help one group of disadvantaged people? Can you mobilize a few people who will join you? Do you know the civic leaders who make decisions about allocating resources? Don't just sit on the sidelines; get involved. Grab a paintbrush, give out backpacks, drive drunks to detox, or pick up a broom. You don't have to meet every need in your community, but you can identify a single injustice or need, ask God to give you wisdom, and then stand tall for those who can't stand for themselves.

CONSIDER THIS...

1. What risks did Stephen take when he cared for needy people? What risks did he face by speaking out boldly about Christ? Would he say it was worth it? Why or why not?

2. Do you think people have become anesthetized to the pain around them? Explain your answer.

3. Who are some marginalized people who are often overlooked in your community?

4. What are some steps your church can take to stand up against injustice? What can your group, class, or circle of friends do? What can you do if no one else will join you?

4 Trust, Even in the Darkness

I can see, and that is why I can be happy, in what you call the dark, but which to me is golden. I can see a God-made world, not a man-made world.

—Helen Keller

Many years ago a devastating earthquake hit Peru. A pastor had been ministering there for many years with his family. His church building collapsed, burying his wife and daughter. When he finally dug them out, both were dead. He was crushed, but he refused to give up on God.

Many years later, I sensed God was leading our church to have a mission in Peru. I sent two men to that country. They asked, "Pastor, what are we looking for?"

I responded, "I don't know, but God will show you."

They landed in Lima, and God led them to the city of Chimbote where they met the old pastor, then 80 years old. He explained their mission as he took them into the desert to meet a nomadic group of South American Indians. The tribe was like the Gypsies in Eastern Europe—despised, forsaken, and abandoned. They needed help . . . a lot of help.

When the men from our church returned to Chicago with their report, I was convinced God had opened a wide door for us to care for the nomadic Indians. Soon a group of fifty of us flew to Peru, taking doctors, nurses, and supplies. When I met the old pastor, the radiance of his faith in Christ was plain to anyone who saw him. Over the next several years we built a school, a church, and a cafeteria in the middle of a desert with no electricity and no running water.

After the earthquake crushed the pastor's church and killed his wife and daughter, he could have shaken his fist at God, but he didn't. He buried his beloved wife and child, got on a donkey, and asked God to use him again.

We may wish for a peaceful, easy life, but sooner or later, virtually every person faces a tragic loss that becomes a crisis of faith. My father-in-law served God faithfully as a pastor for 30 years, but his son was shot in a gang-related fight. I was called to identify the body. My father-in-law's heart was shattered, but he never bailed out on God. He continued to trust Him even in the darkest moment of his life.

When calamity strikes, people reflexively ask hard questions:

—Where was God?

—Does He even care?

—How could God let this happen?

—What did I do wrong?

Some people blame God because they're convinced His love should protect them from suffering. When the disciples were in the boat and Jesus was asleep, a fierce storm threatened their lives. Their desperate question was really a harsh accusation. They woke Jesus and asked Him, "Teacher, don't you care if we drown?" (Mark 4:38) We sometimes smile and shake our heads when we think of the disciples. They were so dense, so slow to believe. But are we any different? Many of us respond to tragedies and threats with the same accusation that God doesn't care or He would have protected us.

Some of us focus the blame on ourselves. We're sure that some sin from the past has finally come due, and we've caused a parent to die, a child to get cancer, or some other problem. Quite often, our assumption of self-blame is totally disconnected to the pain we experience. For instance, a man whose

We sometimes smile and shake our heads when we think of the disciples. They were so dense, so slow to believe. But are we any different?

teenage daughter was diagnosed with lymphoma asked, "What did I do? It must be my fault. If I'd been a better father, maybe this wouldn't have happened to her." He was engaging in magical thinking. He assumed he had done something that caused the sickness, but there was no direct connection between his parenting skills and his daughter's illness. In fact, this man is a wonderful father. However, he felt someone needed to take the heat for his daughter's tragic disease. If it wasn't God, the only option left was to blame himself.

To be sure, some of our problems are self-inflicted. When two teenagers had sex and the girl got pregnant, she complained, "How could God let this happen?" In that case, there *was* a clear connection between a person's behavior and painful events. I don't think God had anything to do with it! Poor choices in finances lead to debt, poor communication leads to misunderstanding and conflict, and eating too much junk food results in weight gain and other health complications. Those connections aren't hard to determine, but sometimes connecting the dots is much more difficult.

Comfort is perceived as a sacred right in our culture. Modern society is full of incredible conveniences and magnificent advances in medicine and technology. As a result, many people—even Christians who study their Bibles—mistakenly conclude that they should be able to control everything in their lives. In reality, they're control freaks with a God complex. When Adam and Eve were in the Garden, their sin was their insistence to "be like God." They wanted autonomy and control, the ability to call their own shots. We're no different today. It takes great faith to realize that some things are simply beyond our control—and even beyond our understanding. That's the lesson of Job.

A RARE FIND

One of the most remarkable conversations in the Bible is found in the opening chapters of Job. Satan appeared in God's throne room and explained that he'd been looking around on the earth to find someone remarkable. God had someone in mind. He asked, "Have you considered my servant Job? There is no one on earth like him; he is blameless and upright, a man who fears God and shuns evil" (Job 1:8).

Seldom in the pages of Scripture does God call a person by name. God must have treasured Job's faith. It amazed Him. As we'll see, Job's persistent and tenacious trust in the face of severe trials was even more impressive.

Every morning Job got up and sacrificed a burnt offering to God. Those gifts were a way for a person to confess, "God, everything I am and everything I have is Yours." Job was saying, "God, here's my marriage, here are my children, here's my business, here are all our possessions, and here's my life. It's all Yours."

God described Job as "blameless and upright, who fears God and shuns evil." Job had integrity. He was complete and whole—spiritually, relationally, physically, and emotionally. His love for God and for people wasn't phony; it was the real deal. He was a devoted father. When he offered sacrifices each day, he wanted to cover any sins his children may have committed. From reading the first paragraphs, we can see they committed plenty of sins! They were living *la vida loca!* They were out all night at clubs partying with their friends. I'm sure Job's heart broke each day as he made sacrifices to cover his kids' sins.

People in Job's community loved and admired him. Job's fear of God caused his relationship with Him to grow stronger. The "fear of the Lord" isn't superficial like a scary movie, and it's not debilitating like a phobia. It's a deep reverence, a sense of wonder at the greatness of God. When John had a vision of the risen Christ, he saw Him in all His glory. How did he respond? He "fell at his feet as though dead" (Revelation 1:17). He fainted! That's a healthy, overwhelming, faith-filled fear of God. With similar reverence for God, Job wasn't complacent in the face of evil. When his children sinned, he took the initiative to make sacrifices to pay for their sins. He wanted his own heart to be pure before God, and he wanted his children to follow his example. Worship wasn't something Job tacked onto his life when he had a few minutes. Praise, gratitude, confession, and humility were woven into the fabric of his character.

How can we tell if we fear God? If we aren't praising and praying, we certainly aren't in awe of His majesty and love—we don't fear Him at all. Today, many people who go to church are just checking the box off their religious requirement to be a good person. When hard times come (and they inevitably will), they panic. They blame God or blame people, including themselves. That wasn't Job's perspective. His fear of God was rooted in a deep understanding of the unsurpassed greatness and wisdom of God. He believed God knew far more than he did, so he was able to trust Him when calamity struck.

Satan didn't buy it. He didn't believe Job's faith was deep and sincere, so he asked for permission to test Job. I can imagine Satan sneering at God's confidence in Job's faith. He demanded:

> "Does Job fear God for nothing?" Satan replied. "Have you not put a hedge around him and his household and everything he has? You have blessed the work of his hands, so that his flocks and herds are spread throughout the land. But now stretch out your hand and strike everything he has, and he will surely curse you to your face" (Job 1:9-11).

God gave Satan permission to take away all of Job's possessions. Before long the bottom dropped out of Job's life. A messenger arrived one day to tell him that a neighboring tribe had stolen all of his oxen and donkeys, the animals that provided the power for his farming operations. Before that news could sink in, three more messengers arrived to tell Job a fire destroyed all the sheep and servants, a raid by the Chaldeans took all of his camels, and a violent wind caused the house to collapse, killing all of his sons and daughters. He lost his ten children, his home, and his business. Talk about a bad day!

Job was heartbroken. He tore his robe in a sign of deep grief, and he shaved his head in remorse. He fell to the ground to pour his heart out to the Lord:

> "Naked I came from my mother's womb,
> and naked I will depart.
> The LORD gave and the LORD has taken away;
> may the name of the LORD be praised" (Job 1:21)

The pattern of Job's life was to worship God and acknowledge that He was in complete control of everything. Job had already committed everything and everyone in his life to God, and now he committed his drama to Him. When trouble came, Job did what he had done every day

Job resisted the temptation to lash out in anger at God or grovel in self-pity. He responded with strong faith because he'd spent a lifetime cultivating his faith.

of his life—he worshiped God. The narrator of the story comments on Job's expressions of grief: "In all this, Job did not sin by charging God with wrongdoing" (Job 1:22). There's nothing wrong with deep sorrow and piercing pain. Jesus experienced the full range of emotions from elation to anger to grief—just like Job, and just like you and me.

Job resisted the temptation to lash out in anger at God or grovel in self-pity. He responded with strong faith because he'd spent a lifetime cultivating his faith. We prepare for temptation well ahead of any difficult event. If we wait until the temptation strikes, we won't be ready, and we'll fall flat on our faces. Some of us open the door to sexual temptations by looking at improper websites and engaging in sensual online conversations. Others of us don't handle money very well. We've been living on the edge of financial collapse for a long time. James said, "Therefore submit to God. Resist the devil, and he will flee from you" (James 4:7). Some of us are sleeping with the devil instead of resisting him! That's not the way to stand strong for God against temptation.

Satan, though, wasn't finished. After Job passed the first test, the devil asked God for permission to harm him personally. Satan was sure Job would curse God then. Soon Satan caused Job to suffer from painful, oozing boils all over his body. In the rest of the story, Job's physical illnesses and problems accumulate: nightmares (7:14), peeling, black skin (30:28-30), disfigurement (2:12; 19:19), bad breath (19:17), severe weight loss (17:7; 19:20), fever (30:30), and unbearable pain (30:17). To lance the festering boils and provide some relief, Job scraped his body with pieces of a broken pot. It was a miserable existence.

In times of great distress, people need love and support. When Job was suffering most, his wife offered this advice: "Are you still holding on to your integrity? Curse God and die!" (Job 2:9)

Probably through gritted teeth, Job responded with a believing heart. He told her, "You are talking like a foolish woman. Shall we accept good from God, and not trouble?" (Job 2:10) Job didn't sin in his response to severe loss, confusing hardship, and now an unsupportive spouse.

God isn't angry when we ask questions in times of trouble, and He isn't upset when we struggle to make sense of things. As long as we move toward Him, He is pleased with us. However, God seldom answers our deepest, most insistent questions. For the next 36 chapters, we read of how Job wrestled with God and with his friends who came to help.

Sometimes it would be better if our friends stayed home. Job's friends did exactly the right thing at first: they wept, tore their robes in grief, and sprinkled dust on their heads to symbolize the transience of life. Then they sat on the ground with Job for a whole week without saying a word. That's what good friends do.

However, those guys weren't willing to keep quiet. They were convinced all the problems could be traced back to Job, and they blamed him for every ounce of his calamity. When he disagreed, they accused him of arrogance. Job couldn't win! Job must have felt terribly lonely and misunderstood during those conversations. Every possession had been wiped out by fire or raids, his dear children had been crushed when their house collapsed in a tornado, his body was wracked by boils and other diseases, his wife told him to give up, and his best friends blamed him for it all. Still, Job wasn't willing to give up on God.

Finally, God showed up. Over and over again, Job had asked, "Why?" God had heard the question, but He gave a very different answer. In fact, when God finally

God invited Job to stop looking at the depth of his problem, but instead, to gaze at the immensity of his God.

spoke, He asked Job a series of questions that demonstrated His complete wisdom, sovereignty, and majesty. He told Job to look at the scope of creation, the incredible diversity of animals, the cycles of seasons, and everything else He has made. He was saying to Job, "You can't understand everything I'm doing, but you can still rely on Me because I'm so much more powerful and wise than you can imagine. Be amazed and trust Me—even in the darkness." God invited Job to stop looking at the depth of his problem, but instead, to gaze at the immensity of his God.

After God overwhelmed Job with the incredible scope of His greatness and wisdom, Job responded with humility and trust:

"I know that you can do all things;
    no purpose of yours can be thwarted. . . .
My ears had heard of you
    but now my eyes have seen you.
Therefore I despise myself
    and repent in dust and ashes" (Job 42:2, 5-6).

Job didn't need to repent because he felt deeply hurt or because he asked a million questions. That's entirely good, right, and acceptable when we suffer loss. And he didn't need to repent for disagreeing with his friends. But he needed to repent of his small view of God. No matter how much we've grown spiritually, we always have a long way to go in comprehending the majesty of God and His rule in our lives. We're finite; He's infinite. He knows all things; we barely see anything. He lives outside of time and knows the end from the beginning; we're grounded in the now. Those were the lessons Job learned when God showed up.

How did things turn out for Job? At the end of the story, we find out: "The LORD blessed the latter part of Job's life more than the first" (Job 42:12). God blessed Job for his faith by restoring his wealth, but I think Job valued something else far more. His new sons and daughters aren't described in the same way as those who died when their house collapsed. These children didn't stay out partying. They followed Job's example and developed a lifestyle of loving, serving, and worshiping God. They were young men and women of integrity. They were the greatest blessing in Job's last years.

AND FOR US

When we face difficulties, what lessons can we learn? God isn't a genie in a bottle that we can rub to get what we want, and prayer isn't a magic wand we can wave to fulfill our wishes. God's purposes are far higher, deeper, and more mysterious than we can imagine, and He refuses to be treated as a magician. Before we can figure anything out, we first need to examine our hearts and our past decisions to see if the trouble is a direct result of our choices.

I talk to people who have lost homes in foreclosures, and they sometimes tell me they have tens of thousands of dollars in credit card debt and two or three mortgages on their homes. They wonder why God let them suffer the loss of their home, but I assure them God had nothing to do with it. The problem isn't God. It's their foolish money management. I've also talked to a lady who was in the hospital to have stents put in her heart. Her doctor had told her for years to watch her diet, to exercise regularly, and to take medication, but she didn't do any of those things. She told me, "Pastor, I don't understand why God would let this happen to me." I tried to keep quiet.

Job's response to suffering shows us how we can trust God in the difficulties we face.

Too often we short-circuit the most important lessons God wants to teach us because we insist on blaming Him or blaming ourselves.

We need to have a higher perspective of our troubles.

Too often we short-circuit the most important lessons God wants to teach us because we insist on blaming Him or blaming ourselves. When trouble comes, we need to think more deeply and trust more fully. We can ask all the questions in the world, but few of them will be answered. The answers simply aren't ours to figure out in this life-time—maybe in the next, but not now.

Paul was amazed at the matchless wisdom and power of God. He knew they are the source of true worship. In his letter to the Roman Christians, he finished a main section of his letter by quoting Job and Isaiah in this explosion of praise:

Oh, the depth of the riches of the wisdom and knowledge of God!
How unsearchable his judgments,
and his paths beyond tracing out!

"Who has known the mind of the Lord?
    Or who has been his counselor?"
"Who has ever given to God,
    that God should repay them?"
For from him and through him and for him are all things.
    To him be the glory forever! Amen (Romans 11:33-36).

We may think we have it all figured out, but such an assumption is dangerous. It implies that we have far more wisdom and knowledge than we actually possess. Instead, the wise course is to bow in humble trust and admit that many things—very important things— are simply beyond our grasp. In the end, Job confessed that his assumptions had been wrong. He admitted his humility and ignorance, and he found real peace.

In his insightful book, *Disappointment with God*, Philip Yancey explains:

By no means can we infer that our own trials are, like Job's, specially arranged by God to settle some decisive issue in the universe. But we can safely assume that our limited range of vision will in similar fashion distort reality. Pain narrows vision. The most private of sensations, it forces us to think of ourselves and little else. From Job, we can learn that much more is going on out there than we may suspect. Job felt the weight of God's absence; but a look behind the curtain reveals that in one sense God had never been more present.[12]

---

12 Philip Yancey, *Disappointment with God* (Zondervan: Grand Rapids, 1997), 264.

Find better friends.

Some of our friends have the grace and wisdom to just be with us when we weep. They know the "ministry of presence" is powerful and appropriate. Eventually, the time to talk and answer questions will come, but not too soon.

When people come and offer advice to help you feel better immediately, don't kick them out. Be kind to them, but you don't have to listen. They're trying to make you feel better fast because they feel uncomfortable with suffering. In most communities, you'll find one or two people, or maybe a support group, who understand, who truly care, and who don't give simplistic, bumper sticker advice. Those wise, gracious people have walked the road of suffering before. They know what you're going through, and they know the long, winding path of healing and hope. Treasure such people. They're God's gift to you.

Stay connected with God—no matter what happens.

Even in his most excruciating pain and confusion, Job didn't bail out on God. He had developed the pattern of worship long before the tragedies struck. He had offered daily sacrifices to God, confessed his dependence on God, and reminded himself that everything belongs to God. When tragedy struck, his heart was strong.

Similarly, our daily dependence on God prepares us to handle unexpected difficulties. Personal Bible study and prayer aren't magic bullets to protect us from harm. Jesus said, "In this world you will have trouble. But take heart! I have overcome the world" (John 16:33). That's a promise! Heart preparation enables us to hold God's hand even when we can't see Him.

Heartaches are often defining moments in a person's relationship with God. We can go one way or the other, trusting Him more than ever or walking away because we blame Him for our trouble. When we're afraid, hurt, and confused, it's not time to abandon our only source of comfort and strength! We can count on Him even when nothing makes sense and no one else is trustworthy.

In times of trouble, open God's Word and read passages that have spoken to you in the past. Sing songs of praise that have lifted your spirits in better times, and pour out your heart to God in prayer. When we suffer, it's human nature to become passive and empty-headed. Fight against that! Fix your mind on the character of God. Let His truth and love melt your heart and energize your body. Don't neglect God when you need Him most.

Hold onto the greatness and goodness of God.

Perhaps the most important lesson to learn from Job is that we need to hold in our hands the extremes of our faith: the unsurpassing greatness of Almighty God and the tenderness of His presence. Theologians talk about God's *transcendence* and *immanence*. He is "far above all" but "as close as our breath." This means that we have a real relationship with God, but He is far more powerful and wise than we can ever know. He's great and holy; we're weak and flawed—but He loves us and calls us His own.

I have a son and two daughters, and I want them to come to me to ask any questions they want to ask. I believe I've earned their respect and their love. Nothing is off limits. They can ask: Why are you a pastor? What are we having for dinner? Why are you going to Peru? What's the President like? What are you getting us for Christmas? The list is endless, and it's wonderful that they feel free to ask anything. It shows they trust me enough to be free with the questions on their hearts. Job was willing to ask the hard questions, and he responded in faith when

God said, "Son, you're asking the wrong questions." After Job heard God's response, he trusted Him even more.

PIERCING QUESTIONS

One of the most difficult questions people ask in times of suffering is, "Where was God?" We can answer that by asking a similar question, "Where was the Father when Jesus suffered and died on the cross?" He was there watching, caring, and weeping. Jesus felt alone and abandoned. He cried out, "My God, my God, why have you forsaken me?" (Mark 15:34) For that moment, the Father let go of Jesus' hand so He could bear the full weight of our sin.

We are never out of His hands, and we're never off His mind. He knows, He cares, and He is at work behind the scenes.

Jesus suffered separation from God for a moment so we never have to be separated from Him forever. This is our confidence: The God of the universe paid the ultimate price to show His love for us, to buy us back from sin and death, and to make us His own dear children. We are never out of His hands, and we're never off His mind. He knows, He cares, and He is at work behind the scenes.

In our church, we don't engage in "happy talk." We're positive and optimistic, but we have a clear view of the sinfulness of people and the tragedies all around us. Genuine hope can't flourish when people are dishonest about the pain and sins in their lives. The grace of God transforms lives, but only when we have the courage to be ruthlessly honest about our desperate need for Him.

Someday we'll have the answers to all our questions. Paul wrote the Corinthians, "Now we see but a poor reflection as in a mirror; then we shall see face to face. Now I know in part; then I shall know fully, even as

I am fully known" (1 Corinthians 13:12). But that day isn't today. We'll have to wait a while to get the answers.

The old Peruvian pastor I met understood the principles in the life of Job. He suffered the death of his wife and daughter, and his church collapsed. Still, he held God's hand and pressed on. He grieved—there would always be a scar in his heart, but a scar is a sign of healing. When I met him, his face was full of love, joy, and confidence. He hadn't wasted years in self-pity, and he hadn't walked away from God. He had no more idea why the tragedy happened than you or I, but he didn't insist on an answer. He was willing to live with the ambiguity and uncertainty of life, hold God's hand, sing praise to Him, and take the next step forward.

Difficulties reveal the inner qualities of a person. If our faith is weak and shallow, it crumbles like Job's house in the wind. However, if our trust in God is cultivated and built over years of consistent worship, it will remain strong even in times of heartache. Our faith doesn't shield us from all of life's problems, and it doesn't prevent deep hurt and grief. A vibrant faith gives us courage to cling to God even in the darkness. Then we can cry out like Job, "I know that my Redeemer lives, and that in the end he will stand upon the earth" (Job 19:25).

How are you handling tragedies in your life?

CONSIDER THIS...

1. What are some losses and tragedies you and your family have experienced? How did family members respond (immediately and later)?

2. Why is the willingness to ask God hard questions far better than blaming Him or blaming yourself? What are the results of each approach?

3. How can we tell if our bad choices have caused or contributed to a time of hardship? How should we respond when we realize we are at least partly responsible?

4. Why is it so important to stay focused on the greatness of God during times of difficulty?

5. Which of the lessons in this chapter do you need to apply today? What difference will it make?

5 Stop Making Noise

Let us not be satisfied with just giving money. Money is not enough. Money can be got, but they need your hearts to love them. So, spread your love everywhere you go.

—Mother Teresa

After we opened the Chicago Dream Center to help women struggling with addiction and prostitution, we realized the ladies who wanted to change their lifestyle should get away from Chicago for a while. They needed a lot of study, reflection, and discipleship to learn a new way of life. God put it on our hearts to buy a farm that's 180 miles away. I didn't want to borrow money to buy it, so I asked God to provide the cash—$160,000. To raise the money, we held a fundraiser to attract interest in the project. We asked people to pledge money to a group of us who agreed to run and bike all the way between the church and the farm in three days.

When the time came for me to hit the street, the weather was unusually hot, and I was sweating profusely. My children gave me a sports drink every two miles so I didn't get dehydrated, but I was miserable. I thought I was going to die before I made it! The entire way I was thinking, *At least this is for a good cause. People will give a lot of money for this!*

When I finished and we counted the cash and pledges, the total came to $12,000. We were a little short: $148,000!

A man who had pledged $1000 to my run also wanted to donate a washer and dryer for our women's shelter. When he and his wife brought us the appliances, he asked about the success of the run. I told him we hadn't raised nearly enough. I took some time to share my heart about the way God could use the farm to reclaim and rebuild the lives of women in our community. The dear couple wept. The man sat up and said, "Pastor Choco, I'd like to give you $50,000, but to get it, you'll need to raise another $40,000 by the end of the year."

It was already December, and I knew families spent a lot of money on gifts, travel, and parties during the holiday season. Every Sunday I reminded our congregation about the generous pledge and the need for matching funds. The money gradually began to come in, yet on New Year's Eve we were still $10,000 short of our goal. At our evening service I told our people where we stood, and I said, "Somebody here has $10,000, and I need it in my hand by midnight. You have three hours."

I waited at the church to see what God might do. Just before midnight a couple came up and handed me a check for $10,000. They said, "Pastor, we've been watching you, and we believe God is with you. We want to help you care for the ladies. Here's the money you need." With their money, the generous gift from the other couple, and other donations we'd received, we were able to buy the farm without borrowing a dime.

When we give generously and selflessly, Jesus is amazed.

TWO PENNIES FROM THE HEART

During the last week of Jesus' life, the crescendo of events came rapidly. He walked into the temple in Jerusalem and cleared out the moneychangers, argued with the religious leaders, and explained what would come in the last days. His disciples were on edge, taking in every moment and every word. Jesus stood up publicly and spoke out boldly day after day. Then the scene changed.

Jesus took His men to the temple, but not to preach or argue with the Pharisees or turn over tables. He led them to a quiet place where they could observe people coming and going. They were in the area where people gave their offerings, and they saw 13 trumpet-shaped brass containers for the people's donations. No one had paper money in those days, and they had no checks or credit cards. They only had metal coins worth various amounts. The containers made noise when coins were thrown into them. The sound was amplified by the architecture of the temple. The acoustics were very good, so even the slightest sound could be heard. The rich people weren't interested in soft sounds when they came forward to make their offering. They wanted to hear the brass clang! The bigger and more numerous the coins, the louder the sound. Mark tells us, "Many rich people threw in large amounts" (Mark 12:41). They made sure everyone heard the big noise and was impressed. For those rich people, giving wasn't worship—it was a show.

She didn't impress anyone in the temple that day—except Jesus.

As the disciples watched, they noticed an elderly woman who wasn't at all like the rich people making their loud donations. She didn't impress anyone in the temple that day—except Jesus. Mark describes the scene, "But a poor widow came and put in two very small copper coins, worth only a fraction of a penny" (Mark 12:42). Jesus had been sitting with His disciples watching the rich people clang their coins into the containers. Mark doesn't provide this detail, but I can picture Jesus nodding toward the old widow as she slowly approached, motioning for His men to sit up and notice. I can also imagine the woman carefully putting her two pennies in the container so they didn't make a sound. As she walked away, Jesus smiled. Peter probably looked at the others with an expression that said, "I don't get it. What's the big deal about her?"

The woman's contribution meant very little to the administration of the temple, but it meant the world to Jesus. He made sure His disciples got the point: "Truly I tell you, this poor widow has put more into the treasury than all the others. They all gave out of their wealth; but she, out of her poverty, put in everything—all she had to live on" (Mark 12:43-44). Her act of faith amazed Jesus, and He wanted her generosity to amaze His men.

Jesus pointed out the stark contrast between the widow and the rich people in the temple that day. They gave to be noticed, to be applauded by their peers. She gave only to honor God. They had given out of their vast surplus. She gave what she needed the most. They didn't miss a thing because they gave. She had given everything she had. She didn't know where her next meal would come from, but it didn't matter. She was thrilled to give her pennies to God. The rich people were part of a corrupt leadership that pressured poor people to give so they could enjoy power and luxury. She was a victim of their abuse of power, but she looked beyond their motives. She gave out of a full heart of love for God.

We need to understand this woman's situation. If she had been a batter in a baseball game, she had several strikes against her. She was a woman in a patriarchal society. Strike one. Her husband had died and left her alone. Strike two. She had no position in society, no investments to fall back on, and no Social Security to serve as a safety net. Strike three. Widows are vulnerable today, but in that culture, their situation was very fragile. All she had was God, but He was plenty for her. The rich people trusted in their wealth, but she abandoned any faith in money. She depended on God for her next meal and her next breath.

In her situation, she could have felt like a helpless victim. If she had, she would have stayed home to sulk. But we see her in the temple giving herself and all her money to the Lord. When she faced hardship, she didn't hoard the little money she had left. She was willing to give it all to the Lord. And there is no indication she expected any kind of reward for her giving that day. Yes, there are promises that God will open the doors of His storehouse if we give, but she gave from a pure heart of devotion—with no expectations and no strings attached. The loud noise of the rich people's contributions may have resonated in the ears of the people in the temple that day, but the subtle sound of the widow's pennies captured the heart of Jesus.

> The loud noise of the rich people's contributions may have resonated in the ears of the people in the temple that day, but the subtle sound of the widow's pennies captured the heart of Jesus.

FULL HEARTS, OPEN HANDS

We live in a very materialistic society. People today expect to have the best of everything—a nice car, the latest electronics, a fine home, tailored clothes, and every other diversion and convenience. If we're not careful, we can lose our grip on what's really important. That's the message Jesus was giving His disciples as they watched people make their contributions. Today, giving to churches and nonprofit agencies is down. We can blame this fact on the poor economy, but donations were declining even before the economy went south. We're simply more self-absorbed than ever before.

When people give, they often have mixed motives: They feel guilty if they don't give, they want to be known for their generosity, they're grateful for all they have, or they want to make a difference in the lives of others. Many people don't give much or don't give at all because they don't see any connection between their hearts' desires and God's kingdom. They cling to every dime because they want to spend it all on themselves. In fact, they resent any insinuation that they should give their precious money to God. If they were honest, they'd say, "Why should I give any of my money to God? I earned it, didn't I? It's mine, and I'll use it any way I want."

To some extent, all of us have mixed motives. The reasons to give fall along a spectrum from altruism to egoism. *Altruism* is the desire to give aid or increase the pleasure of others. It's outward directed. *Egoism* is self-directed; people give to rid themselves of guilt or win applause from others. They're looking for the personal benefits of giving. In the scene at the temple, the rich people were giving out of egoism, and the woman was altruistic. Jesus wanted His men to notice the difference. Let's look at some lessons the widow teaches us.

Give gladly and quietly.

The promises of God's blessing for our giving are powerful incentives, but Jesus is looking for something deeper, something more important to Him: the willingness to give without expecting anything in return except the pleasure of expressing devotion to God. In His most famous sermon, Jesus taught,

> "Be careful not to practice your righteousness in front of others to be seen by them. If you do, you will have no reward from your Father in heaven. So when you give to the needy, do not announce it with trumpets, as the hypocrites do in the synagogues and on the streets, to be honored by others. Truly I tell

you, they have received their reward in full. But when you give to the needy, do not let your left hand know what your right hand is doing, so that your giving may be in secret. Then your Father, who sees what is done in secret, will reward you" (Matthew 6:1-4).

The disciples were listening to the Sermon on the Mount that day. A few years later, just before He died, Jesus showed them a perfect example of what He had taught on the side of

> **When we give to win applause from others, we forfeit God's applause.**

the hill. In the temple, they watched as a widow gave two pennies in secret, with no fanfare and no demand to be noticed. But God had noticed, and He was smiling.

Our hearts are deceptive. It's easy to think that giving generously is always noble and pure, but it's not. When we give to win applause from others, we forfeit God's applause. I know some people who make sure their friends know how much they give to the church and other causes. They brag, and they hope people are impressed. But Jesus said they've received all the reward they're ever going to get. They won't hear, "Well done" from Him. In Mark's account of Jesus and the disciples in the temple, Jesus points to a poor widow, but we never know her name. That's the point. She wouldn't want it any other way.

No matter how many strikes we have against us, we need to stay connected to God.

The woman was old, her husband had died, she had no source of income, and she was an outcast in her male-dominated society. She was fragile, but she didn't sulk in self-pity, and she didn't stop giving because she had so little. She got up, went to the temple, and gave to the Lord. In the same way, we may have a lot of strikes against us. We may have lost a job, a house, or someone we love. We may feel like giving up, but we need to get out and go to church. We may not have a lot of joy to give, but we can give all we've got. We may not have much insight to give, but we can share what we have with others. We may not have much money, but we can give with the assurance that Jesus notices.

Ludwig van Beethoven was one of history's most gifted composers, but later in his life, he became deaf. His inability to hear caused him to feel awkward in social settings. One day he learned a friend's son had tragically died, so he hurried to his friend's house. He was overcome with grief, and he didn't know how to express his love for his friend. He saw a piano in the room. He walked over and played for half an hour, pouring out his emotions with elegance, beauty, and power. When he finished playing, he left. Later his friend remarked, "The visit of no one else had as great an impact on me. Beethoven gave all he had, which was his music."

Paul had a lot to say to the Corinthian church about giving. Among other things, he told them, "For if the willingness is there, the gift is acceptable according to what one has, not according to what one does not have" (2 Corinthians 8:12). In other words, it's not the size of the gift that impresses God; the thing that thrills God is the size of the person's heart that moves him to give as much as he can.

We can give without expecting or demanding anything back, even in tough times.

This is what impressed Jesus about the widow's gift. During a famine and drought in Israel, God fed the prophet Elijah by sending ravens with bread and meat. When the brook dried up, Elijah moved on to the

STOP MAKING NOISE   115

village of Zarephath near Sidon where he found a widow living with her son. The famine was severe in their area, too. The woman and her son had exhausted their supplies. Elijah asked her for some bread and a drink of water.

"As surely as the LORD your God lives," she replied, "I don't have any bread—only a handful of flour in a jar and a little olive oil in a jug. I am gathering a few sticks to take home and make a meal for myself and my son, that we may eat it—and die" (1 Kings 17:12).

Elijah asked her to trust God even when she had almost nothing left, and she did. She gave with no expectations that God would bless her, but God honored her faith and provided flour and oil for them for the duration of the drought.

We realize that Jesus gave us far more than we can ever give back to Him.

Jesus stepped out of the glory of heaven to live, walk, and sacrifice His life for us on earth. If we're reluctant to give, if we try to hold on to everything we've got, or if we give to be noticed by others, we've entirely missed Jesus. Paul quoted a beautiful first-century song in his letter to the Philippians. The song describes the life of Christ in three movements: His humility, His sacrifice, and His exaltation. We won't sacrifice without humility, and the Father won't exalt us unless we gladly sacrifice.

Paul wrote,

> Have the same mindset as Christ Jesus:
> Who, being in very nature God,
>> did not consider equality with God something to be used
>> to his own advantage;
> rather, he made himself nothing
>> by taking the very nature of a servant,
>> being made in human likeness.
> And being found in appearance as a man,
>> he humbled himself
>> by becoming obedient to death—
>> even death on a cross!
> Therefore God exalted him to the highest place
>> and gave him the name that is above every name,
> that at the name of Jesus every knee should bow,
>> in heaven and on earth and under the earth,
> and every tongue acknowledge that Jesus Christ is Lord,
>> to the glory of God the Father (Philippians 2:5-11).

Are you amazed at Christ's gift of grace to you? Do you feel overwhelmed by His love, forgiveness, acceptance, and mercy for someone as undeserving as you? If you do, you'll be a generous and cheerful giver. You can't help it.

In his detailed letter to the Corinthians, Paul outlined several motives for them to give. He explained that their gifts would help people who were suffering from famine, they would set a good example for other Christians, and God promised to bless them. But all of those reasons are secondary. The first and most powerful motivation to give is when our hearts overflow with gratitude because they're filled with the incredible grace of Christ. Paul wrote, "For you know the grace of our Lord Jesus Christ, that though he was rich, yet for your sakes he became poor, so that through his poverty you might become rich" (2 Corinthians 8:9). If we give to earn recognition from people, it's selfish. If we give to gain leverage with God so that He owes us, we're fools. The reason we give is because Christ gave Himself to us, and we're amazed at His generosity.

I believe God tests our sincerity in many different ways, but one of them is when we experience financial difficulties. When we suffer financially, we need to take a look at how we've been spending, saving, investing, and giving. If we've made unwise decisions, we need to make some changes. But if we suffer a financial setback when we've been faithful to manage our money and give to God's kingdom, God is testing our motives. Do we get angry that "the system isn't working"? Do we blame God for not coming through on His promises? Or do we look into our hearts and conclude, "I've given gladly with no strings attached. God will provide again in His way and His timing." That was the widow's motivation. Is it yours and mine?

We need to abandon our trust in money to fulfill us, and trust only in God.

It doesn't matter if we're rich or poor, money can become an idol in our hearts.

The widow in the temple could have held those two pennies in her hands in a death grip, but she went to the temple to give them to the Lord. It doesn't matter if we're rich or poor, money can become an idol in our hearts. Rich people thirst for more; poor people want some because they believe it will fill the hole in their hearts. It won't. True riches come in knowing and loving Christ.

God wants us to be wise with our money. We can save as much as we can, spend as little as possible, and invest in our retirement, but we shouldn't put our highest hopes in those things. Our hope should only be in God. Only God is ultimately faithful and true.

Giving is one of the ways we worship God. If we're stingy and grudging, we may write the check or put a Benjamin in the offering plate, but we won't be glad to give. God loves it when people can't wait to give. He's happy when they tell Him, "I'm so glad to get to play a small role in building Your kingdom! Thank You so much for all You do for me!" When we're gripped by God's grace, we won't resent every penny we give. Instead, we give Him everything we possibly can. Gratitude revolutionizes our giving. After all, Jesus gave His all for us. If we have any idea of the magnitude of His grace, we can't wait to give back to Him.

Ultimately, we give to God, not just to the church.

I hope you're in a church where you trust the way money is handled. I hope your church is pouring money into effective outreaches and ministries of social justice to care for the poor. Flawed human beings, though, lead all churches, so we can't demand perfection. When we give, we first give ourselves to God, and then we give our money to Him. The widow was willing to donate all she had to a corrupt religious establishment led by men who would kill Jesus, but her heart wasn't fixed on them—it was fixed on God.

We can be sure Jesus is watching us.

When we're in church, He sees when we're texting a friend instead of paying attention to the message. When we're at work, He notices when we do our best even when our boss isn't around. When we're at home, He's thrilled when we give focused attention to our spouse and kids instead of getting lost in a television program or a computer game.

The benefit of altruistic giving isn't fuller pockets. It's the sheer joy of knowing our gift delights God.

And Jesus notices our generous, selfless giving. The widow didn't have any idea Jesus and His men were in the corner watching her that day, but we know He's watching us. When we give out of full hearts and open hands, we can be sure He elbows some angels next to Him and whispers, "Did you see that? Pretty cool, huh?"

The benefit of altruistic giving isn't fuller pockets. It's the sheer joy of knowing our gift delights God. The widow gave to God and His kingdom. She experienced the thrill of living on the edge of her faith, giving all she had with no demands, and trusting God to use it any way He chose.

THE PAYOFF

The man and his wife who gave $10,000 to complete the offering for the farm aren't wealthy people. The money they donated was most of their life savings. This couple and the ones who donated $50,000 may not have seen God bless them financially because they gave, but they sit up and take notice when they hear stories of God changing women's lives at the farm. They're thrilled with every testimony of a life transformed, children reconciled with their mothers, and new directions of hope and love. That's their payoff, and they feel they've been richly repaid.

CONSIDER THIS...

1. What are some good reasons people give to the Lord? What are some wrong motives?

2. What can you do when you realize you have impure motives for giving?

3. How do you think the disciples responded when Jesus showed them the contrast between the rich people and the widow?

4. What difference does it make to start with focusing on Christ's gift of grace to us before we think about giving back to Him and His cause?

5. What are some reasons Jesus was so impressed with this lady?

6. What are some ways you can choose to be like her in giving?

6 Go Deeper

The greatest enemy of Christianity may be people who say they believe in Jesus but who are no longer astonished and amazed.

—Mike Yaconelli

A woman in our church came to me with a problem. She complained, "Pastor, I'm going to leave my husband. I can't stand to live with him any more!" I asked her to explain, and she told me, "He's driving me crazy. He's more interested in sports than me. When he comes home each day, he turns on a sports channel and watches television until he goes to bed." She paused for a second, then she exploded, "I just can't stand it!"

I asked, "Is he beating you or abusing you in any way?"

"No, nothing like that."

"Is he harming your children?"

"No, Pastor. He wouldn't do that."

"So," I tried to get under the surface, "you don't find it fulfilling or convenient to live with him any longer."

Her eyes lit up. "Yes, that's it exactly!"

I talked with her about the covenant of marriage and the commitment she had made to God on their wedding day: "To have and to hold

God is faithful. If He gives me a week, I'll live it for Him. If He gives me a year, it's His. If He lets me live to be an old man, I'll praise Him every day. I belong to Him, Pastor.

from this day forward, for better for worse, for richer for poorer, in sickness and in health, to love and to cherish, till death us do part." She didn't want to hear what I said, but she stayed in the conversation. After a while, the Spirit worked in her heart, and she melted. As she cried, she told me, "It would be a lot easier to walk away. For a long time, I've tolerated my husband, but I haven't loved him the way you're talking about. I'm not sure I can do that, Pastor."

"With God's help," I reminded her. "You can with God's help."

We talked about the steps she could take to overlook some of her husband's annoying behavior, forgive genuine offenses, and take the initiative to communicate respect to him. She assured me she'd try. A few weeks later, I saw her in church—with her husband. He had never come before. After the service, she found me and said, "Pastor Choco, I can't thank you enough for encouraging me to stay with him. I've had to trust God more than ever, and He's done a miracle. Did you see my husband here this morning?"

We face many problems that look too big and too difficult for us to face. At times it seems easier to give up. In the face of doubt and darkness, only Spirit-powered courage enables us to trust God.

Philip is a man in our church who was having some health problems. For months, he hadn't felt very good. Finally, he went to the doctor. When the tests came back, the doctor gave him the dreaded news: "You have cancer, and you probably have only a year to live." Philip was shaken. He didn't want to leave his wife and children, and he didn't want them to go through the agony of watching him die a slow, painful death. He could have gone into a cocoon of anger, doubt, and self-pity, but he chose to trust God. He told me, "God is faithful. If He gives me a week, I'll live it for Him. If He gives me a year, it's His. If He lets me live to be an old man, I'll praise Him every day. I belong to Him, Pastor. He can do with me whatever He wants. That's the legacy I want to leave my wife and kids."

Philip's faith encouraged me every time I saw him. Week after week and month after month, he relied on the sovereignty and goodness of God. He didn't demand a long life or a painless death. He put himself in God's gracious hands. Instead of dying a year later, he lived twelve years—years that were filled with love, laughter, and wonderful times with his family. Philip served in the church all those years, and I never heard him complain. His trust in God amazed all of us who watched him.

Carl and Rachel had been faithful members of our church for many years. They both served in a variety of ways. Every Sunday morning at 6:30, Carl showed up to help set up the auditorium for worship. Two years ago his company went through financial difficulties and downsized. That's a sanitized word for "layoffs." They let Carl go with a week's notice. He immediately began looking for another job and put out dozens of résumés. For months, all he got were rejections as he and Rachel lived on her small salary from a part-time job. Times were hard. They held onto their house for a long time, but finally, they lost it in a foreclosure. During these difficult months, Carl and Rachel didn't get angry with God and they didn't blame each other. From the day Carl got the news he was unemployed, they determined to go deeper with God, trusting Him more than ever before and finding hope in a seemingly hopeless situation.

Charlie and Shari were having problems with their teenage son, Matt. He had been a good kid when he was younger, but recently he had become withdrawn and resentful. They had tried to connect with him, but he blew up in a rage and stomped off to be alone in his room. One day Shari noticed the corner of a plastic bag hanging out of Matt's backpack. She pulled it out, and she saw a white powder. She took it to Charlie. He put his finger in the powder and then to his tongue. It was cocaine. They confronted Matt, and he denied it was his. For months, the family lived in tension so thick you could cut it with a knife. At times, Charlie wanted to strangle his son, and at times, Shari wanted to act like nothing was wrong.

They went to a pastor for counseling, and they learned some new skills about relating to an addict. They conducted an intervention, and Matt exploded. Their message, though, had gotten through. A few weeks later, he realized he was wasting his life. The jury is still out on Matt's future, but Charlie and Shari are determined to trust God every second of every day. They haven't given up on God because their beloved son became an addict. They're learning to lean on Him more than ever.

No matter how hopeless a situation appears, God has the power to work a miracle. The first step, though, often is the hardest to take. When we feel like giving up, we need to hang on with all our might.

ON THE SHORE

One day as Jesus preached on the shore of the Sea of Galilee (which Luke calls the Lake of Gennesaret), two fishing boats were nearby. The fishermen had fished all night, but they hadn't caught any fish. They were washing their nets, which they did after every fishing trip—fish or no fish. After washing them, they'd stretch them out to dry so they'd be ready for the next trip.

Jesus got into one of the boats, the one belonging to a fisherman named Simon. He asked Simon to row the boat a short distance away from shore. Jesus then sat down and spoke again to the crowd. The acoustics of His voice on the water made it easier for the people to hear Him. When He had finished His message, Jesus turned to Simon and said, "Put out into deep water, and let down the nets for a catch" (Luke 5:4).

Most of us aren't fishermen, so we don't understand the impact of Jesus' instruction to Simon. His directions were absurd. Fishing was a nighttime activity. It was now broad daylight. But that wasn't the only reason Simon might have thought Jesus' instruction was ridiculous. Jesus was a carpenter and a rabbi, not a fisherman. Who was He to tell a seasoned professional how to do his job? In addition, fishing the previous night hadn't proven successful. Simon's response was a mixture of brutal reality and hesitant hope. He said, "Master, we've worked hard all night and haven't caught anything. But because you say so, I will let down the nets" (Luke 5:5).

In his mind, Simon surely had plenty of questions. He may have caught the glance of his fishing buddies that said, "What's that guy thinking?" But he chose to obey Jesus. They rowed into deeper water. Simon motioned to his partner to help him cast the nets. They probably expected the nets to remain motionless, but suddenly they felt the tug of fish. Then the pull became so strong they could barely hold the nets in their hands. The fish pulled so hard the nets began to break, so they called for friends to bring another boat to help them. In a few minutes, both boats were so full of fish that they began to sink!

Simon's attention suddenly switched from the fish to the One who had given the order to go fishing. He looked at Jesus and fell on his knees in the boat—in the middle of the biggest haul of fish he'd ever seen—and told Him, "Go away from me, Lord; I am a sinful man!" (Luke 5:8)

All the men—Simon (also called Peter) and his partners, James and John—were astonished. They realized they'd witnessed a genuine miracle. Jesus, though, wasn't interested in flopping, slimy fish. He had bigger things in mind. He told Simon, "Don't be afraid; from now on you will catch men" (Luke 5:10). The men rowed their boat to shore and immediately left behind the biggest catch of their lives to follow an even bigger catch: the promised Messiah.

The spiritual life of Simon Peter is much like yours and mine—it had a lot of ups and downs. Sometimes he was clueless, but on other occasions he got it magnificently right. After the disciples had watched Jesus heal countless people and teach about the kingdom hundreds of times, He asked them, "Who do you think I am?" Peter responded, "You are the Christ, the Son of the Living God" (Matthew 16:16). That's right, Peter.

But Peter is also known for making one of the biggest blunders in the Bible. On the night Jesus had His last Passover meal with His men, they noticed something was missing. The wine was there, the bread was on the table, but the Passover lamb was missing. Or was it? The lamb wasn't *on* the table because it was sitting *at* the table. Jesus again explained that He was going to die to pay for the sins of the world. Peter insisted on joining Jesus. He said, "Lord, why can't I follow you now? I will lay down my life for you" (John 13:37). A couple of hours later when soldiers came to arrest Jesus, Peter tried to kill one of them with a sword. He was a fisherman, not a swordsman, so he missed. He cut off the man's ear instead, which Jesus reattached, but that wasn't the worst of Peter's mistakes that night.

During the last hours before Jesus was arrested, a whirlwind of conflicting thoughts and emotions filled the disciples. All week they had watched Him win verbal fights with the angry religious leaders, and they had argued about who would hold the top positions in Jesus' cabinet when He set up His kingdom. Now He was being arrested, tried, and sentenced as a traitor. Things weren't working out like they planned! If the authorities killed their leader, the disciples were understandably afraid they'd come after His closest followers—them! At the moment Jesus was arrested, most of them ran, but Peter and John followed the soldiers as they took Jesus to His first trial.

Peter stood in the cold courtyard outside the hearing, warming his hands near a charcoal fire. As he waited to see what would happen, the bold fisherman's courage wilted. Hours earlier at dinner, he had proclaimed his undying loyalty to Jesus, but when a little girl asked him if he was one of Jesus' followers, Peter shot back, "I don't know Him." Two more times, common people asked Peter if he was connected to Jesus, and he denied Him. After the third time, Jesus looked at Peter, and the fisherman realized he had betrayed the Lord of glory. He walked away and wept bitter tears (Luke 22:62).

On that terrible Friday when the sky became black as night, the disciples thought the world was coming to an end. For them, that's how it felt. All their dreams were shattered. Saturday must have felt like a long, slow death. The One they hoped would set up a new kingdom was dead and buried, and they had nowhere to go. They felt hopeless and alone.

On Sunday morning, they were shocked when some women ran to tell them they'd seen Jesus! Could it be true? They didn't dare hope. Then Jesus himself appeared to them. He had come through the walls, but He wasn't a ghost. In the presence of the resurrected Christ, they were equally thrilled and terrified. For several weeks, Jesus appeared to them many different times, but at least one of the group believed that his previous betrayal had forfeited Christ's love. The rest may have felt that Jesus had reinstated them, but not Peter, who had betrayed Him three times after swearing complete loyalty.

One day several of the disciples were together, and Peter told them, "I'm going out to fish" (John 21:3). The others agreed to go along. This idea wasn't like you or me choosing to have a fun day at the lake. Peter's statement meant more than that—a lot more. He was giving up on Jesus, on his role as a disciple, and on any hope of finding meaning again. He was bailing out on Jesus and going back to the one thing he was sure he could do: go fishing.

When we feel like we can't go on, when we hit a dead end, when we believe a failure has ruined our lives, we often go back to an activity that feels most familiar.

When we feel like we can't go on, when we hit a dead end, when we believe a failure has ruined our lives, we often go back to an activity that feels most familiar. When the children of Israel struggled for years in the desert, they gave up on Moses and God. They wanted to go back to Egypt. They said, "At least there we had free fish and lots of vegetables" (Numbers 11:4-6). Yes, the food was free—because they were slaves! Peter went back to fishing, but others of us may bail out on God and go back to drinking, to climbing the corporate ladder, to being numbed by entertainment, to illicit sexual pleasures, or to a city where we feel at home. But wherever we go, God can get our attention and remind us of His love and purpose for our lives.

The guys fished all night, but they caught nothing. In the early morning light, a man appeared on the distant shore and yelled to them to cast their nets "on the right side of the boat." This instruction was absurd, but it sounded strangely familiar. They did what the man suggested, and they caught a huge number of large fish. Peter suddenly realized what was happening. He yelled, "It is the Lord!" He jumped into the water and swam to shore before the men in the boat full of fish could get there.

When Peter stepped onto the beach, Jesus was cooking some fish on a fire—a charcoal fire. When they finished eating, Jesus asked Peter three times, "Simon, son of John, do you truly love me?" The sights, sounds, and smells of the moment reminded Peter of his biggest sin: He had betrayed Jesus three times. The smell of the charcoal fire reminded him of the three painful conversations a few weeks before when he had told a little girl and two others that he didn't even know Jesus. Was Jesus being cruel by reminding him? No, He was extending grace to the deepest recesses of Peter's sin. We have an almost limitless capacity for self-deception. Jesus needed to remind Peter of the depth of his sin so he could experience the height of Jesus' forgiveness. Humility is the sure pathway to repentance, which then leads to joy.

When Peter was in the boat and saw Jesus on the shore that morning, his heart melted. He had bailed out on Jesus, but Jesus hadn't bailed out on him. Peter jumped into the water as a kind of baptism of commitment. He wanted to be immersed in Jesus, to be completely devoted to Him because he sensed Jesus' amazing love. When he got to the shore, Jesus completed the process of exposing and forgiving his sin. Finally, the fisherman was a whole, complete man of God. He was finally ready to fish for men.

JUMPING IN

The bookend scenes of boats and beaches in Peter's life help us understand some important spiritual principles.

Don't settle for shallow.

When Jesus found Peter washing his nets, his boat was in the shallow water. In fact, the bow may have been pulled onto the shore. The shallows are where life requires no risks, but they also offer no adventure. Plenty of people orchestrate their lives to avoid risk at all costs. Certainly, wisdom leads us to avoid stupid risks, but a full and meaningful life can't exist in the safety of shallow water. Jesus told Peter to go deeper, and He's inviting us to do the same thing.

Many of us carefully craft our lives for maximum comfort. We buy the latest electronics and use modern conveniences. We choose cars with the most advanced technology, and we sit in recliners with a brand name that reminds us we're lazy. Everything we do is designed to make our lives easy, but living this way makes life empty and meaningless. The people who populate God's Hall of Fame in Hebrews 11—Noah, Abraham, Joseph, Moses, David, the prophets and others—didn't settle for comfort and ease. They heard the call of God to go into deeper waters—to trust Him to use them to change the world—and they said, "I'll go!" A world is dying and going to hell just outside our doors, and in some cases, inside our homes. God is calling us to step out of our complacency and self-absorption, to engage friends and family members, to reach out to care for those who are lost and hurting, and to trust Him to use us to transform lives. Yes, this kind of life costs something, but it delights God and enriches our lives.

> They heard the call of God to go into deeper waters—to trust Him to use them to change the world—and they said, "I'll go!"

Dag Hammarskjöld was the Secretary General of the United Nations and a strong Christian. He summarized his view of life in a simple but profound statement: "For all that has been, thanks. For all that will be, yes."[13] He was willing to answer Jesus' call to go into deeper waters.

Don't give up.

If Jesus didn't give up on Peter, He won't give up on you or me. Peter's denial of Jesus wasn't much different from Judas's betrayal. Judas hanged himself in shame; Peter was so depressed he went fishing. Peter had been on the Mount of Transfiguration and had seen Moses and Elijah there with Jesus, but when a little girl called him out as a disciple, he denied even knowing Him. Jesus, though, wasn't finished with Peter. His forgiveness extends to all people, no matter how badly or how often they've sinned, no matter how hopeless they feel, no matter how bleak their future looks.

A young woman began attending our church several years ago. She was beautiful and wild, but she agreed to become part of our discipleship program called Chicago Master's Commission. Elizabeth and I invited her to live with us for nine months so we could encourage her. For several years, she took steps forward and then steps backward. We poured ourselves into her, pled with her, confronted her, and loved her, but she didn't seem to get it. Several people wanted to give up on her, but I knew she had a spark of greatness in her. No matter what happened, we kept our door open for her. Finally, her spirit broke. Like Peter on the shore with Jesus, this young woman has never forgotten where she has come from, but she always is amazed by God's grace to forgive and restore. Today she has answered God's call to go deeper and is one of our worship leaders.

---

13 Journal entry by Hammarskjöld, published in 1964.

In the fall of 1941, England had been at war with Nazi Germany for two years. Things had begun badly, but a few military victories were finally giving the British people a new sense of hope. In October of that year, Prime Minister Winston Churchill was asked to speak at Harrow, the school of his boyhood. His address that day demonstrated his fierce tenacity. He told them,

> I am addressing myself to the School—surely from this period of ten months this is the lesson: never give in, never give in, never, never, never, never—in nothing, great or small, large or petty—never give in except to convictions of honor and good sense. Never yield to force; never yield to the apparently overwhelming might of the enemy. . . . Do not let us speak of darker days: let us speak rather of sterner days. These are not dark days; these are great days—the greatest days our country has ever lived; and we must all thank God that we have been allowed, each of us according to our stations, to play a part in making these days memorable in the history of our race.[14]

Earlier when the war was going against England, many members of Parliament were very critical of Churchill's policies, and some wanted him to surrender to Hitler's Germany. Churchill would have nothing of it. With bulldog tenacity, he refused to quit even when the news was bleak and many people had lost hope. Today he is often considered "the greatest man of the twentieth century." Why? Because he refused to quit.

---

14   Winston Churchill, speech to Harrow School, October 29, 1941, cited at www.winstonchurchill.org/learn/speeches/speeches-of-winston-churchill/103-never-give-in

Every difficulty, every form of opposition, and every doubt is a test to see if we'll quit or grab God's hand and take the next step forward. Tests are a normal part of the Christian life, just like they're a regular and necessary part of the curriculum in schools. Tests force us to study and

Every difficulty, every form of opposition, and every doubt is a test to see if we'll quit or grab God's hand and take the next step forward.

learn the most important lessons. When we face difficulties, God hasn't forgotten us. He's put us in a position to learn a lesson we'd learn no other way.

Sandwiched between the two stories of the catches of fish is another dramatic moment for Peter and Jesus on the lake. One night Jesus sent the disciples ahead in a boat. The wind and waves threatened to sink them, but then they saw Jesus walking on the water toward them. They were terrified, but Jesus reassured them, "Take heart; it is I. Do not be afraid" (Matthew 14:27). Peter's courage overcame his fear, and he asked if he could join Jesus on the waves. I'm sure Jesus smiled as He waved for Peter to get out of the boat. The fisherman had been on the water countless times, but he had never been *on* the water like this! He passed the boldness test, but like many of us, his courage quickly evaporated. He looked around at the wind and waves, and his doubts caused him to sink. Jesus again rescued him, and when the two water-walkers got into the boat, the disciples were amazed. That night, Peter was like many of us—he passed one test with flying colors and blew the next one. Even then, Jesus took his hand. He wasn't going to let him drown. He had a lot more for Peter to do.

Sometimes our tests occur because we're not devoted and obedient. We drift into attitudes and behaviors that are like an acid drip in our souls, slowly corroding what's valuable. But some tests come because we're running full on and full out for Jesus. Satan shoots arrows of criticism to try to stop us. No matter what the test may be, we need to pay attention and pray, "Lord, what do you want me to learn from this?" He's an incredible teacher . . . if we'll just listen and obey.

Don't let past failures determine your destiny.

From the human perspective, Peter had every reason to give up. He had failed as miserably as anyone in history by denying he even knew the Lord of life who was on His way to the cross. For weeks, Peter was haunted by the undeniable fact that he had cowered in fear when Jesus had the courage to face the most relentless enemy: death. Even when Peter ran away to go fishing, Jesus pursued him there. When Jesus assured him of His forgiveness, He gave him a new mission: to feed His sheep. The fisherman was to become a shepherd of God's people. The history of the early church shows that Peter was the chief spokesman to proclaim the gospel of grace, and he was a miracle worker who demonstrated God's power. He was the leader of the new movement of those who followed The Way. Jesus didn't let Peter's past failure ruin his glorious destiny.

I see this pattern played out in countless lives. When Jesus captures someone's heart, things are never the same again. Alcoholics have wasted their lives and hurt those they love, but when they are redeemed, they become beacons of forgiveness and hope for everyone they know. Single moms may have felt alone and abandoned, but they find a community of believers who give them support and encouragement and they raise their kids to be spiritual champions. Hundreds of prostitutes have left the streets of our community and experienced the transforming power of God's love. Abused children grow up, are healed by the grace of God, and become the most compassionate and wisest people I know. The list is almost endless. God seems to delight in rescuing those who seem most lost by changing the hearts of people our culture has discarded. It's the way of the cross.

A couple of years ago, I was asked to speak at a prison in Chicago. As I began, I scanned the faces in the room and noticed someone I knew. He was a young man who had been coming to our church. When our eyes met, he looked very ashamed. While I spoke, he looked down the whole time. After I finished, I went over to him, smiled, and said, "We'll talk later." He nodded. I found out he was doing 90 days for drinking and driving. When he got out, he came to church and found me after the service. He apologized for his sin, and I assured him of God's forgiveness. Many people would have let the shame drive them away from church, but not this brave young man. He faced his sin and repented. Since his release, he and his wife have been faithful members at our church.

Accept Christ's forgiveness.

Being honest about sin takes a lot of courage. It's a lot easier to deny we did anything wrong, blame others, or sulk in shame. We don't like it when the Holy Spirit points out our selfish attitudes and destructive behaviors, but He's shining a light in the darkness for our good. The only way to experience Christ's wonderful cleansing is to admit we're dirty. As long as we insist we're clean, we remain blind and filthy—and we stink. Jesus didn't just forgive Peter; He pursued him. When Peter ran, Jesus found him. When Jesus showed up, He spoke the fisherman's language. Jesus performed the same miracle

> Jesus didn't just forgive Peter; He pursued him.

He had done three years before when Peter first saw Jesus. I can imagine Peter had a flood of memories of their time together between the two miraculous catches of fish. Jesus let Peter smell the charcoal . . . to remember his betrayals. With the smells and memories fresh in Peter's mind, Jesus graciously forgave him.

Jesus pursues us, too. His Spirit convicts us of our sins and present selfishness—not to crush us, but to restore us. But first, we have to be honest about what we've done. Confession is agreeing with God about our sin and about His complete forgiveness. John promised, "If we confess our sins, he is faithful and just and will forgive us our sins and purify us from all unrighteousness" (1 John 1:9). Author and pastor Frederick Buechner notes, "To confess your sins to God is not to tell God anything he doesn't already know. Until you confess them, however, they are the abyss between you. When you confess them, they become the bridge."[15]

Dive in!

No excuses. No blaming others. No playing it safe. When Peter was at his worst, he realized Jesus had come after him. In his joy and relief, he dove into the water. Nothing else mattered but being close to Jesus. He left the other men in the boat to wrestle the net full of fish. He swam for shore as quickly as he could. He didn't care who thought he was crazy. He just wanted to be near Christ.

Are you and I thrilled with Jesus? Are we amazed at His love, forgiveness, and acceptance? Do we look around to see who might think we're crazy if we raise our hands in worship, or are we free of

---

15   Frederick Buechner, *Beyond Words* (HarperOne: New York, 2004), 65.

self-consciousness because our minds and hearts are full of Him? Peter didn't dive in only because he had right theology or he cherished certain religious practices. He dove in because he knew the love of Jesus.

Paul valued sound theology, but he knew there's more to life than that. In a prayer in his letter to the Ephesians, he wrote,

> I pray that out of his glorious riches he may strengthen you with power through his Spirit in your inner being, so that Christ may dwell in your hearts through faith. And I pray that you, being rooted and established in love, may have power, together with all the Lord's holy people, to grasp how wide and long and high and deep is the love of Christ, and to know this love that surpasses knowledge—that you may be filled to the measure of all the fullness of God (Ephesians 3:16-19).

Paul was praying that the Christians in Ephesus—and us, too— would dive into Christ's love. When we do, our world turns right-side up.

Answer Christ's call to fish for people.

Peter knew all about fishing for fish, but he had a lot to learn about fishing for people's souls. He and the other disciples spent three years as apprentices, watching Jesus care for people, preach the gospel, teach the crowds, argue with those who opposed him, live for the Father, and die for the lost. Peter's spiritual life was checkered with many ups and downs, but Jesus was looking for obedience, not perfection. He was looking for people who might wrestle with their choices, but who ultimately would choose to become agents of change.

When Peter cast nets out of his boat, he never knew what kind of fish he'd catch. In the same way, we cast our nets and bring in anyone:

prostitutes, business leaders, gangbangers, city officials, rich people, poor people, powerful people, weak people, drug addicts, religious leaders, and anyone else who responds to the message of Jesus.

We won't catch fish if we keep our boats tied to the dock, and we won't catch anything if we stay in safe, shallow water. If we want to catch fish, we need to go into deeper waters. Yes, there are dangers there. We'll face storms and long hours of hard work, but God will bring fish into our nets, even if we haven't caught anything for a while. Like Peter and his friends, we'll see the miracle of fish in the nets only when we let Jesus into our boats. We trust Him to guide us, equip us, and use us, and we trust Him to bring the people to us so we can capture them with love.

Both of the miracles of big catches of fish happened after nights of failure.

Both of the miracles of big catches of fish happened after nights of failure. When times are tough, when we don't see any miracles of changed lives, we need to welcome Jesus into our boat. The fish don't come to us by magic. We still have to do the hard work of fishing, but Jesus produces the catch.

TO THE END

Disappointments don't have to define us. An inconsistent life isn't a reason to give up on ourselves because, in fact, God hasn't given up on us. No matter how far Peter fell, Jesus reached down to find him. No matter how far Peter ran, Jesus went there to assure him of His love and forgiveness. Peter's response to Jesus demonstrated amazing faith. You might ask, "How?" Certainly, the scenes we've examined—on the shore when he had given up on fishing, when his doubt caused him to sink after he walked on water, when he denied three times that he even knew Christ, and when he bailed out completely and went fishing with his friends—show spectacular and repeated failures, but Peter demonstrated amazing faith by accepting Christ's forgiveness each time and coming back to Him.

When we look at Peter's life from boat to boat and from one miraculous catch to the other—and beyond into the early church—we realize that Jesus didn't let Peter's repeated failures prevent him from having a rich, full, meaningful, and effective life. Years before the final scene on the shore, Jesus had seen into the future. He told Peter, "Blessed are you, Simon son of Jonah, for this was not revealed to you by flesh and blood, but by my Father in heaven. And I tell you that you are Peter, and on this rock I will build my church, and the gates of Hades will not overcome it" (Matthew 16:17-18).

If Jesus was willing to build His church on Peter's declaration of faith that Jesus was the Son of God, what does He want to build on yours and mine?

CONSIDER THIS...

1. What are some ways people respond to personal failure? Which ones lead to the experience of forgiveness and hope? Which ones lead to discouragement and more destruction?

2. In what ways can you identify with Peter's ups and downs?

3. What are some reasons people give up too quickly? Which ones often tempt you to give up? Explain your answer.

4. Why is it important to realize Jesus pursued Peter when he was at his worst? How does this insight encourage you?

5. What would it look like for you to dive into your relationship with Jesus?

7 A Few Crumbs

God is God. Because He is God, He is worthy of my trust and obedience. I will find rest nowhere but in His holy will, a will that is unspeakably beyond my largest notions of what He is up to.

—*Elisabeth Elliot*

Rebecca came to church every week with her two children, Robert and Maria. Things were tough at home. Her husband, William, had a good job, but he was seldom available. He lived for sports. He followed every game in every Chicago season: the Cubs, the Bears, the Bulls, and the Blackhawks. Both kids suffered from neglect, but especially Robert. By the time he was in junior high, his parents' marriage was in shambles and he felt abandoned. A divorce eventually finalized the estranged relationships between William and the rest of his family.

In high school Robert became deeply depressed and withdrawn. He hated his father, and he unfairly blamed his mother for the separation. Rebecca tried to talk with him and help him grieve his deep hurts, but he always pushed her away. He was a walking volcano. Like Mt. Vesuvius, his rage was dormant most of the time, but when it blew, it devastated everyone around him.

Rebecca didn't know what to do. She tried everything. She showed Robert a lot of love, but he just ignored her. She tried being strict to control his behavior, but he became furious and violent. She sent him to a counselor, but there was no change. She asked her parents to keep him for a summer to see if it would help. When he came home and started the new school year, his withdrawal and rage were worse than ever. He would often express suicidal thoughts. At home, he defied his mother in every conversation. Two teachers called Rebecca to tell her they were having trouble with Robert in their classes. If things didn't improve, the school would have to suspend him. The only person who didn't incur Robert's wrath was Maria. He loved his sister, but she was terrified of him and kept her distance. William could have been a positive influence, but he was already living with another woman and didn't want to be bothered by Rebecca's pleas for help. The kids were an inconvenience for him.

On several occasions, Rebecca called me to come over to her house. Her voice was shaking. "Pastor, I don't know what to do! Robert is throwing things and cursing me. I've tried to talk to him, but he's completely out of control. Can you help?"

When I arrived at the house, I could see the rage in the young man's glare, and I saw tears streaming down Rebecca's face. Maria was hiding in her room. "Pastor," Rebecca almost whispered, "I don't have anywhere to turn. I'm trusting God for a miracle."

EVEN PUPPIES

After a couple of years of ministry, reports about Jesus had spread throughout Judea. In fact, people in the pagan regions also heard the news about a man who had incredible powers. A woman who lived near the coast in the pagan district of Tyre and Sidon (today's Lebanon) had heard those stories. She secretly hoped Jesus would come to her city because she had a need—a desperate need. Jesus and His men went to that region to escape the constant pressure of ministry in

Galilee, hoping to get some rest. When the woman heard the news that Jesus had showed up in her community, she found him, barged into the house where He was staying, and poured out her heart: "Lord, Son of David, have mercy on me! My daughter is demon-possessed and suffering terribly" (Matthew 15:22).

Imagine what this mother experienced each day. Demon possession isn't just having a bad day. It occurs when a demonic spirit, a fallen angel with terrible powers, indwells a person. The evil of hell is unleashed in the victim with devastating results. This little girl's face would have been contorted in snarls and grimaces as the demon commandeered her vocal cords and spoke with a voice that wasn't hers. Her sweet personality would be replaced with deception and hatred. The other women in the community must have whispered about the troubled mother and refused to let their kids play with her daughter. The kids in town surely were ruthless in making fun of the little girl. Both of them, the mother and her tragic daughter, were outcasts. Their lives were a disaster! How would you respond if you saw your dear little girl under this kind of evil spirit? Author and pastor Tim Keller comments about the mother's courage in going to Jesus,

> You know why she has this burst of boldness, don't you? There are cowards, there are regular people, there are heroes, and then there are parents. Parents are not really on the spectrum from cowardice to courage, because if your child is in jeopardy, you simply do what it takes to save her. It doesn't matter whether you're normally timid or brazen—our personality is irrelevant. You don't think twice; you do what it takes. So it's not all that surprising that this desperate mother is willing to push past all the barriers.[16]

---

16   Tim Keller, *King's Cross* (Dutton: New York, 2011), 86.

The woman was a Canaanite, a pagan who would have lived in the shadow of the temple of Eshmun, a god of healing. But Eshmun couldn't heal her daughter. We can imagine how many times she pleaded with Eshmun, but her dear daughter still suffered. Then she heard about another God, the God of the Jews, the promised Messiah, the Son of David. If only He'd come . . . .

This mother may not have been to Bible class to understand all the teaching about the nature of the Messiah, but she'd heard enough to convince her that Jesus was the real deal. However, when she cried out to Him for help, Jesus ignored her. She didn't let this stop her. She kept pleading, begging, and imploring Jesus to relieve her daughter of the demon that was cruelly ruining her life. In fact, she begged so long and so loudly the disciples became annoyed. Now it was their turn to beg. They cornered Jesus and whined, "Send her away, for she keeps crying out after us" (Matthew 15:23).

Jesus responded, "I was sent only to the lost sheep of Israel" (Matthew 15:24).

Was Jesus being heartless and insensitive? Not at all. His first priority was to show the nation of Israel that He was the fulfillment of all the prophets' promises. He was well aware that the covenant with Abraham was to bless all the nations of the world, but He was first sent to Israel, and then they were to take the message of the gospel to everyone else. After His resurrection and just before His ascension, He told His followers to be His witnesses "to the ends of the earth" (Acts 1:8). God's heart is always tender toward the foreigners, the downtrodden, the outcasts, and all those who have no hope. Going first to the people of Israel was a strategic plan, not a value statement about the other people in the world.

This mother wasn't willing to take "No" for an answer. She knew she had only one shot. It was a big surprise—a wonder of grace—that Jesus left Israel and came to her city.

She came over to Jesus, got on her knees, and cried, "Lord, help me!"

He certainly wasn't going to come back anytime soon! In her request, she didn't claim any rights or make demands. She didn't use self-pity, and she didn't manipulate Jesus in any way. She came over to Jesus, got on her knees, and cried, "Lord, help me!" At this point in the conversation, she didn't appeal to Jesus as the Messiah of the Jewish nation. She now had a wider view. She acknowledged Him as Lord, the Creator of all things, including all the nations of the world . . . even her daughter.

Jesus turned to her and replied, "It is not right to take the children's bread and toss it to the dogs" (Matthew 15:26).

The Jews sometimes called Gentiles "dogs," an insult intended to be the worst kind of slam on them. In that day, packs of wild dogs roamed the land killing livestock and scavenging off dead animals. However, that's not the word Jesus used in this instance. He chose the word for "puppies," the pets that lurk around our dinner tables waiting for scraps to fall on the floor (or for kids to reach down and feed when the parents aren't looking).

The woman's response was magnificent. She still didn't back down, nor did she play the role of an angry, demanding victim. She simply pleaded with Jesus by using His own metaphor. She replied (maybe with a smile), "Yes it is, Lord. Even the [puppies] eat the crumbs that fall from their master's table" (Matthew 15:27).

She appealed to God's vision to reach the whole world with the gospel of grace. She acknowledged the central role of the Jewish nation in God's plan, but she reminded Jesus (as if He needed to be reminded) that even the puppies get to eat what falls on the floor, and she wanted a few crumbs for her daughter!

Jesus must have beamed at her reply. I can imagine Him leaning back and laughing out loud when He told her, "Woman, you have great faith! Your request is granted" (Matthew 15:28). Her daughter was freed from the demon at that instant.

When Jesus made this comment, he may have looked directly at Peter. As we saw in a previous chapter, Jesus had walked on water on a stormy night. When Peter saw Him, he asked if he could step out on the waves, too. Jesus agreed. When Peter stepped out of the boat, he was bold at first, but fear gripped his heart and he began to sink. He cried out, "Lord, save me"—almost the same words as the plea from the Canaanite woman. When Jesus pulled Peter out of the water, He told him he had "little faith." Now he was telling a Gentile woman with a demon-possessed daughter—someone who had no claims at all on the Messiah's attention but wouldn't take "No" for an answer—that she had "great faith." This mother punked Peter!

It's very interesting that the two events when Jesus expressed amazement at a person's faith involved a centurion and a Canaanite woman. The Jews despised Gentiles as a group, but these two had great faith in Jesus. Biblical scholar James Edwards writes about this mother:

> She appears to understand the purpose of Israel's Messiah better than Israel does. Her pluck and persistence are a testimony to her trust in the sufficiency and surplus of Jesus: his provision

for the disciples and Israel will be abundant enough to provide for one such as herself. . . . What an irony! Jesus seeks desperately to teach His chosen disciples—yet they are dull and uncomprehending; Jesus is reluctant to even speak to a walk-on pagan woman—and after one sentence she understands his mission and receives his unambiguous commendation . . . . How is this possible? The answer is that the woman is the first person . . . to hear and understand a parable of Jesus . . . . She is the first person in the Gospel to *hear* the word of Jesus to her.[17]

The disciples had tried to send her away. They too probably considered all Gentiles to be dogs (in the insulting sense), and they may have wanted to protect Jesus from being bothered or defiled by contact with a pagan woman. Also, they were men in a patriarchal society: They saw women, especially persistent women, as nuisances. The disciples didn't grasp the heart of Jesus, but she did. He was first dedicated to the people of Israel, but He cared for every person on earth. When this mother kept coming, Jesus opened the door of His mercy and answered her request.

DEMONS IN OUR FAMILIES

I've talked to plenty of parents like the Canaanite woman. They've watched a daughter pull away from them and get involved with a young man who is clearly using her for sex. They've seen a son quit trying at school because he's gotten involved with a crowd doing drugs. They've

17   James R. Edwards, *The Gospel According to Mark* (Eerdmans: Grand Rapids, 2002), 221.

witnessed their child changing from sweet and compliant to sullen and furious. When these moms and dads talk to me, they describe something very much like demon possession: snarling or apathetic facial expressions, voices that are filled with hate instead of love, and personalities twisted by evil and sin. They ask, "What happened to my dear child?" "Where did my wonderful son go?" "What's going on in her head?" In tears, they often tell me, "Pastor, this isn't the child I taught to ride a bike. What happened?"

Our kids may be under the evil grip of gangs, sex, pornography, depression, lying, bitterness, or any other force that seems to possess them and rob them of sanity. When this happens, we can try other gods. We can try ignoring the problem and hope it will go away; we can try to put the clamps on our kids and angrily demand compliance without discussion; we can ship them off to a rehab clinic or a grandparent's house; or we can simply give up in despair. To be sure, confrontation and control might be *part* of the solution, but they aren't the *ultimate* answer.

When we trust anything more than God, we make it an idol, a false god. If we care more about our reputations as "good parents" than our kids' welfare, or if we value peace and quiet more than honesty and resolution, we're pursuing false gods. There's another option: We can turn to the Messiah and fall at His feet to beg for help. If we're desperate enough, and if we've given up on other gods, we may have only one option left: Trust Jesus or watch our kids self-destruct. When we trust Him, He'll give us wisdom and peace, and He'll give us direction to address the problem with grace and strength.

Our faith in God isn't magic. We don't utter an incantation or follow some ritual and hope for the best. Instead, we push away the fog of doubt and hurt, and we focus on the majesty of Christ. He's the Creator, the sovereign Lord of the universe, and the One who keeps His covenant of grace with those who trust Him. If our kids won't go to church, they aren't beyond His reach. God isn't limited by time and space. The story of the Canaanite woman's daughter is the second case in the Gospels when Jesus healed from a distance. He still does.

If your child is under evil influences, let me offer a few suggestions.

Identify the demon.

A son or daughter may, in fact, be possessed by an evil spirit, but in the vast majority of cases, evil comes in the form of a child being consumed and controlled by peers, drugs, sex, or anything else that produces a spirit of rebellion or apathy. Don't overlook the signs, and don't rationalize or minimize established patterns of destructive behavior. I've talked to parents who laughed at their son's lying, stealing, and drug use, and they say, "Oh, boys will be boys." Yes, and boys become addicts, get girls pregnant, are arrested, and throw their lives away, too. Call the behavior out. Be honest, but stay under control. When Jesus confronted people who were possessed by demons, He never lashed out or was agitated. He was in complete control because He trusted His Father to give Him wisdom, power, and love. That's a good example for us, too.

Take the initiative.

Be a student of your child, even at an early age. Every person has a God-given "bent" of talents and personality. Our role as parents isn't to make them grow up to be just like us, but to nurture them and direct them so they become all God wants them to be. The apostle Paul told dads to avoid "exasperating" their children. We exasperate them by neglect or over-control. Avoid extremes and give them plenty of love, instruction, and affirmation.

Even the best of kids go through that dark time of biochemical transformation—adolescence. They can change almost overnight, and it's confusing for everybody. During this time, don't withdraw, don't blast, and don't withhold affection. Stay involved, give clear directions, and enforce the consequences. They may tell you they hate your involvement, and they may demand "their space." Don't believe it. Clear, loving, firm parenting gives them a sense of safety when their world is in chaos. It's essential for their mental and emotional health—and for yours, too.

Some parents feel intimidated by psychologists who tell them they need to give their kids plenty of room and autonomy. I take the opposite point of view. I tell my kids that as long as they live under my roof, everything in the house is under my authority: their closets, their backpacks, their wardrobe, their computers, and their cell phones. When children realize they can't keep secrets, it may annoy them at first, but they usually realize they can trust an authority who knows everything about them and loves them unconditionally—including Jesus and their parents.

No matter what happens, hang tough.

Parents need to claim their authority in their homes. Authority doesn't imply permission to abuse, but to powerfully and lovingly guide the children. The Canaanite woman could have abdicated her authority. When other mothers gossiped about her and her daughter, she could have become isolated and depressed. When other gods couldn't help her, she could have thrown up her hands and quit. When the disciples tried to run her off, she could have felt hopeless. But nothing caused this mom to quit. She had bulldog tenacity and the heart of a lion. She claimed her authority as a parent, and she then claimed Jesus' authority as the Lord of all. She trusted God when no one else even cared.

Nothing was easy for the Canaanite mom. She had a dozen strikes against her as a woman, a Gentile, an outcast in her own culture, and a daughter whose condition caused her crippling emotional pain each day. But she refused to give up—even when Jesus seemed distant and His disciples tried to run her off. Nothing could keep her from falling at the feet of Jesus to beg for His help.

Appeal to God's mercy.

The Canaanite mother didn't appeal to her position in society, to her own authority, or to her moral record. Those, she instinctively understood, didn't count with Jesus. Instead, she looked outside herself. She pleaded with Jesus first because she was convinced He was the Messiah, the Son of David, and then because she realized He was the Lord and Creator. In addition, she believed God's ancient covenant with Abraham extended all the way to her living room. The "master's table" may have been set for God's chosen people, but "all peoples on earth will be blessed through" Abraham's descendents (Genesis 12:3). She may not have been a Jew, but she was a human being who was a recipient of God's global promise.

We may feel confident of our status and talents at work or in our neighborhoods, but when we're desperate for God to work a miracle, we no longer trust in our abilities. We stretch ourselves out on the mercies of God. We can't change a heart, but He can. We can't turn prodigals toward home, but He can bring them to a point of repentance. We can't produce fruit out of a dead tree, but He can. We can't make water flow in a desert, but He can. Nothing is impossible with God.

REBECCA'S MIRACLE

I went to Rebecca's house several times to try to calm down her enraged son. My presence seemed to help, but not for long. Finally, I realized more drastic action was necessary. One night I asked Rebecca to leave the room. "I want to have a man to man talk with Robert," I explained. She nodded and went into another room in the house. I turned to Robert and said, "Young man, God has something very special for you. You're deeply hurt by your dad, but that's not going to determine your identity or your destiny. I want to invite you to participate in a challenging, life-changing program for young men just like you. Are you willing?"

Robert was initially hesitant, but as I explained more about Chicago Master's Commission, our church's discipleship program, he warmed to the idea. He knew high school students whose lives had been radically changed. He knew I wasn't just blowing smoke when I told him God could work wonders in a young man's life to provide peace and purpose. Finally, he agreed to enter the program.

Rebecca was elated, but I wanted to bring her expectations down to earth. I told her, "Do you remember Jesus' disciples?" She nodded, and I continued, "There was a John who became 'the beloved disciple,' but there was a Judas who betrayed Him, a Thomas who doubted, and a Peter who talked big but didn't follow through in the clutch. I don't know which one Robert will be, but we'll do our best to inject God's love and power into his life."

In the program, I got to spend some time with Robert. I told him about the pain of my father walking out on us, and he could relate to every word I said. I explained that the hurt of losing a dad is deep, but God is "a Father to the fatherless." As we talked, and as he met more young men who were responding to Christ, Robert's defiant heart melted, and he trusted Jesus to be his Savior. Gradually, his hatred faded away. He realized his rage had controlled his life—and it threatened to destroy the things most precious to him: his relationship with his mother and sister.

As Robert read the Bible and talked to new friends, he realized God had a challenging, inspiring plan for his life. He had something to live for—a person and a cause bigger than himself. He apologized to Rebecca for being such a pain. She wept and hugged him so hard he thought he'd pop. Her dear, loving, laughing child had come home. He told Maria he was sorry for causing her to be afraid of him. She told him, "No problem. That wasn't really you."

Robert decided to follow God's call to ministry and enrolled in a second year of Chicago Master's Commission. When he graduated, an amazing thing happened. His list of people to invite to the ceremony included someone he hadn't seen in a long time—his dad. That day his father came and sat with Rebecca and Maria. When Robert crossed the platform and received his diploma, his father stood and cheered with them. Months before, Robert had written his dad a long letter to tell him that he forgave him for not being there for him and Maria. He didn't hear from his dad until the day before graduation when William called to say he was coming. Forgiveness had already happened; now, reconciliation could begin.

Rebecca had faced her son's demons of abandonment, hatred, drugs, and depression, and she hadn't stopped trusting God even when she saw no progress for a long, long time. The Canaanite woman kept begging Jesus to cast the demon out of her daughter, and eventually

He answered her request. In the same way, Rebecca kept begging Jesus to rescue Robert from the demons in his life. And finally, Jesus came through. Robert was recently anointed to serve as an associate pastor for our youth ministry and as a leader in Chicago Master's Commission.

If you're a parent, don't delegate raising your kids to others. I know there are some single mothers reading this, and I'm not trying to heap guilt on them. They face incredible pressures to make life work without a man at home, but they need to find a way to make their kids a priority. They can look for programs in the church that are designed to help single parents, and they can find friends who will encourage them and help them find resources. If the dad isn't involved, find a good and godly man to show love and be a good example to your child.

Every person faces plenty of distractions today. Being a parent is hard work. It's a lot easier to invest time in people and things that aren't as demanding as kids. Distractions are dangerous. All parents need to stay connected to their kids and disciple them to become fully devoted followers of Jesus Christ. This process doesn't just happen. It takes time, sweat, and heart, but it's the most rewarding job in the world.

If you notice significant changes in your child's behavior, don't panic, but look for patterns. When kids are in junior high and high school, hormones and peer pressure can cause wild fluctuations in mood. Don't worry about a bad day, but a bad week is a concern, and a bad month is a huge red flag.

By the time a child reaches junior high, the demons are everywhere, but kids often don't have the perception to notice them or the skills to combat them. At this age, many kids drift away from their parents and from God. Today, children are busier than ever, and they're more vulnerable to being hurt by friends. Insecurity makes them easy prey for peers who don't have their best interests at heart. If parents have kids in junior high, they shouldn't put their relationships on cruise control. Instead, they need to increase their involvement and initiate conversations about the things that their kids are facing: sex, peer pressure, grades, purpose, dating, sports, lying, and a host of other topics.[18]

When kids are in high school, our relationship with them changes again. They're preparing to embark on the adventures of marriage and mission. Our task is to equip them to be successful adults. When the apostle Paul picked Timothy to be his disciple, he gave him increasing responsibility, and he gave him clear directions about how to fulfill God's calling in his life. Paul's two letters to Timothy are models of love and dedication to a young man learning to walk with God and have an impact on others. Those letters are a wonderful blend of tenderness and tenacity, of affirmation and direction—the kind of relationship parents can have with their older kids. At that age children are quickly becoming young adults. Parents who *neglect* their kids produce young adults who feel angry and insecure. Parents who *smother* their kids with directions and control create young people who lack confidence in their ability to respond to life's challenges. High school and college students need an accurate perception of their talents so they can hone them for the future, and they need to increasingly own their responsibilities and become productive members of the body of Christ—in the church and in the workplace.

Whether families live in the inner city, in the suburbs, or on a farm, the primary responsibility of parents is to equip their kids to walk with God for a lifetime. Quite often, parents feel unqualified for this task, and they come to it with deep hurts of their own. There are lots

---

18   Parents can find useful "Conversation Starters" at www. realworldparents.com/starters/.

Desperation isn't a bad place to be . . . unless we forget about God.

of pressures and distractions, but there are no excuses. It's our God-given privilege to raise up our kids "in the discipline and instruction of the Lord." When we're old, we won't miss the new dress or car or fishing rod we didn't buy because we invested time and money in our kids. We'll look back with gratitude that we valued our kids, and we'll wish we'd done even more.

Desperation isn't a bad place to be . . . unless we forget about God. Raising kids is one of the hardest jobs in the world. Almost every mom and dad feels helpless and hopeless from time to time. When you come to the end of yourself, fall at the feet of Jesus and demonstrate amazing faith in His love and authority to work in your child's life—and your life, too.

CONSIDER THIS...

1. How have you seen a parent be incredibly courageous in caring for a child?

2. What are the demons in children's lives today? (Think about grade school, junior high, high school, and beyond.)

3. What had the Canaanite woman heard about Jesus that prompted her to trust Him so fervently? If you had been her, would you have quit when Jesus didn't pay attention, when the disciples tried to get you to leave, or when Jesus said He had other priorities? Explain your answer.

4. If you're a parent, what do you think it means to disciple your children using authority and love?

5. If you're a young person, how are you avoiding the demons in your world?

6. If you're an adult but not a parent, what are situations in your life that parallel with the desperate faith of the Canaanite woman?

8   Redirected

The world has yet to see what God can do in, for, by and through a man whose will is wholly given up to Him.
—D. L. Moody

In the world of politics, you must always have control—or at least the perception that you have it all under control. Control your message, control the money, and control the mobilization of people. There isn't a politician alive, past or present, who wouldn't admit that control equals power. Politicians get inspired to take on great causes, but most of the time they eventually resort to compromising positions. The fear of political backlash stops most politicians in their tracks, and they compromise just enough to get through the next election instead of going above and beyond.

Billy was an alderman in Chicago for sixteen years. He always felt that he had control and was going above and beyond the call of duty because he was taking a stand for his community. His list of accomplishments and achievements was long and impressive, but despite the influence, accolades, power, and money, he always felt a void in his life. Billy filled the emptiness with worldly possessions, drinking, and women. There wasn't a door that wouldn't swing open for him at any hour of the day or night. As long as he moved his chess piece the way the powers-that-be stipulated, he was at the top of his game. One false move, however, and he would fall off the board.

When Billy became an alderman, it appeared that he was in control and had it all, but in reality, he lived an empty life. During that time he and his wife got a divorce. After partying on the weekends, he retreated to his nice single-family home to recover from the hangovers. Most people didn't know he often broke down in tears because he felt lonely and depressed.

Throughout his life he always felt alone, despite having a loving family and numerous friends. Clearly, something was missing in his life. In his pursuit to fill the emptiness, he married his second wife Veronica, had children, and changed his unhealthy lifestyle. He continued to search for something more. He didn't understand how an influential man with a great family, stable finances, and a bright political future could continue to feel lonely.

The last time Billy ran for alderman, it felt forced. In his heart he knew he didn't want the role and responsibilities anymore. As the election approached, he had to make his rounds to ask for votes. One Sunday morning he was scheduled to be at our church at 10:45 A.M., but at 11:00 he was still sitting in his car outside. When he finally came inside, one of our ushers escorted him to the first row. He appeared to notice nothing and no one. He was caught up in a mental cloud. His mind seemed to drift in and out of the service.

Billy heard me acknowledge his presence as I asked the church to pray for him. While everyone prayed, he also prayed silently. Being raised Catholic, it was a new experience for him to see all the members of the church praying, rejoicing, and worshiping with excitement and enthusiasm. He felt an overwhelming sense of peace as he prayed. He knew that something had to change in his life. He prayed for God's help.

When we finished praying, Billy suddenly felt as though the cloud had lifted, and he began to see the loving, prayerful people all around him. At the end of the service, he politely scuffled his way out of the church, shaking hands along the way. He was eager to call his wife and explain what he had just experienced. As soon as he made it to his car, he enthusiastically told her that he had found a church to join.

Politically, Billy always thought he had done the right thing for the people in his community. After sixteen years, however, each passing day became more cumbersome, and he grew tired and disillusioned with the job. His embitterment created more anguish and inner turmoil. Seeking to be loyal to those in authority over him, he had never rocked their boat. He simply did what was expected of him.

Billy pursued justice through the eyes of Jesus.

As his faith was nurtured and he started to focus on God, Billy's life began to change. He started to pray and seek pastoral counsel before he made decisions in the political arena. Billy previously had fought for social justice issues, but now it was different. He no longer weighed the political costs or implications. He was no longer concerned about how much press or notoriety he could receive. Billy pursued justice through the eyes of Jesus. This purposeful decision made him very unpopular in the eyes of other politicians, but he didn't care. He was no longer indebted to man, but to God. He was no longer willing to compromise for political expediency or to appease the political power brokers. He knew that there was no turning back to what he used to be. He made a decision to walk in complete faith regardless of the cost.

As a result, Billy and his wife suffered. People started questioning and mocking his new beliefs and his newfound friends. But as it turned out, God was purging and pruning their lives to prepare them for new growth.

During this time, the newly appointed Illinois governor asked Billy to join his senior staff. After much prayer and counsel, Billy decided this was a great chance to start fresh, and he seized the opportunity. He became the number one Latino in state government, but his new journey came at a huge price. As an alderman, he had been at the top of his game. He was the President of the Latino Caucus, Chairman of the city's Human Relations Committee, and heavily involved with the Obama Presidential campaign. When Billy chose to work for the governor, he was at peace with his decision, but other politicians and leaders weren't pleased that he hadn't consulted with them or obtained their approval before he acted.

As a result, he lost many things, including powerful friendships and the ward he represented and loved. Billy and Veronica also lost their powerful positions and their home. Although this was one of the hardest things they've had to face, they put their trust and faith in God. Beyond everything they lost, God gave them peace. Billy gave up control—not to man, but to God. He no longer felt alone. God wanted to take them on a different journey by breathing life into them and using their experience to help others.

REDIRECTED

The new sect wouldn't go away. The Jewish leaders had been annoyed by Jesus' teaching and miracles. As His popularity grew, they decided to get rid of Him. Their plot began to take shape early in His career (Mark 3:6), but they couldn't move too quickly because so many people believed He was the true Messiah. Finally, they'd had enough. One of Jesus' followers conspired to hand Him over to them. Judas was paid thirty silver coins to betray the Creator of the universe. Guards arrested Jesus in the dark of the night and dragged Him through a series of mock trials. Lying witnesses presented false evidence. The testimony was obviously contrived, but the religious leaders didn't care. They convicted Jesus and sent Him to the Roman governor for execution. Later that day, Jesus died a horrible, public, shameful death on a wooden cross. As far as the religious authorities were concerned, it was done. Things could go back to normal.

But three days later, rumors began to circulate in the city that Jesus wasn't dead. The guards at His tomb reported that an angel had rolled the stone away and Jesus had come out alive! Weeks passed, and more reports of sightings spread throughout the city. Then, about seven weeks after the crucifixion, one of His followers spoke to a crowd on the feast day of Pentecost, and thousands believed his message! Things were really getting out of hand. The Jewish authorities were outraged. They looked for every opportunity to arrest members of the new sect— especially the leaders. Battle lines were clearly drawn. It was now us against them. There would be only one winner and one loser. In situations like this, the ones in authority feel threatened, and they react with fierce vengeance toward anyone who gets in their way.

When some men in an obscure synagogue picked a fight with Stephen because he was telling people Jesus was the Messiah, the Jewish authorities realized they had a golden opportunity to make a point. They arrested Stephen and charged him with treason. Stephen, though, didn't back down an inch. In fact, he called them "stiff-necked" unbelievers! Those weren't just *fighting* words. They were *dying* words. The sophisticated, educated, austere religious leaders turned into a mob.

They grabbed rocks to throw at the young man to kill him. To be able to throw harder, they took off their robes and laid them at the feet of one of their top leaders—a man named Saul.

Saul of Tarsus wasn't just on their team; he was the quarterback, the captain, the All-Star in the most prestigious Jewish leadership group in the nation. He had studied under Gamaliel, the most acclaimed scholar in the land. Saul was the top dog, so he had the most to lose if this new faith in Jesus became popular. He wasn't going to let that happen.

After Stephen was executed, the Christians in Jerusalem scattered. We can imagine the sneer on Saul's face when he realized he had them on the run. But it wasn't enough that they'd left his city. If they were still alive, they could cause problems wherever they went. He asked for extradition papers so he could travel to other cities to capture them and bring them back to Jerusalem for trial and execution. For Saul, this wasn't just a job. He was passionate about snuffing out the new group of Christ followers. Luke describes him as "still breathing out murderous threats against the Lord's disciples" (Acts 9:1). Kidnapping, mock trials, and murder. Those are the actions of a cornered wild animal—a person who will use any means to stamp out his opposition.

Saul left for Damascus, a city about 135 miles north of Jerusalem, because he heard some of the Christians had fled there. He and his detachment of soldiers were on a "search and destroy" mission. The arrest warrants they carried were like IEDs (improvised explosive devices) to destroy the believers they found.

Saul was a gifted leader. He was dedicated, smart, and driven. If he were in business today, we'd see his picture on the cover of *Fortune* or *Money*, or maybe *Time* or *Newsweek*. He was supremely confident in himself and his mission. Like many self-absorbed, driven, gifted leaders, it took a big crash to humble him. Hardened hearts often require a sledgehammer of grace.

As Saul and his party neared Damascus, a light suddenly flashed around them. It was broad daylight, so the light must have been extraordinarily bright and blinding. He fell to the ground in fright and heard a clear, compassionate, firm voice: "Saul, Saul, why do you persecute me?" (Acts 9:4)

Saul immediately realized this wasn't a dream. He hadn't eaten bad pizza for lunch, and it wasn't some kind of optical illusion. He was a Pharisee who believed in the supernatural appearances of God. This was one he'd never forget! He understood that God was speaking to him just as He had spoken to Moses through the burning bush. The voice called his name twice. When we find a name repeated in the Scriptures, it's just like a loving mom or dad talking to a child with great sincerity and tenderness. But it may also signify that Saul was moving so fast that Jesus called his name twice to get his attention.

Saul's voice probably trembled when he asked, "Who are you, Lord?"

The voice spoke, "I am Jesus, whom you are persecuting. Now get up and go into the city, and you will be told what you must do" (Acts 9:5-6).

Saul saw the risen Lord. Could it be true? Was it really Jesus? The One who had been executed . . . the One who was reported to be still alive after he was killed . . . the One Stephen had said was the Messiah and the fulfillment of all the prophets? Saul had been in the middle of all this. His passion and his mission were to annihilate the fledgling Jesus movement. Now Jesus was talking to him!

Jesus accused Saul of persecuting Him—not the church, not individual believers, but Jesus Himself. Jesus identifies completely with each person who trusts in Him. If someone gives us a drink of water, it's like giving it to Him. If someone falsely condemns us, it's the same as slandering Him. With Jesus and His followers, it's always personal—very personal.

The men with Saul saw the blinding light and heard a sound, but they only understood Saul's side of the conversation. They must have been very confused! Saul had fallen to the ground at the sight and sound of Jesus. When Jesus left, he got up, but he couldn't see a thing.

His men led him to Damascus. For three long days, Saul sat in darkness without eating or drinking anything. We can only imagine what was going on in his mind during those days. Had he really seen and heard Jesus? Yes, it was unmistakable. Why didn't Jesus zap him on the spot? That's what he deserved! How could he have been so wrong for so long about Jesus? What would his friends and colleagues in the Sanhedrin say when they heard the news? Would he be blind forever? I'm sure he thought about the stones hitting Stephen as he stood and watched him die. And he probably remembered Stephen's last words asking God to forgive his executioners, a prayer just like Jesus prayed on the cross. As Saul sat in darkness, the light of spiritual insight began to grow.

> Proud people have to be broken, and defiant people need the grace of deep, radical conviction.

Proud people have to be broken, and defiant people need the grace of deep, radical conviction. In the days when Saul was in Damascus alone, God's Spirit was producing this conviction. In the darkness, Saul realized how blind he had been. His arrogance began to melt into genuine humility. He had been driven to kill those who threatened him, but Jesus had reached out to show His love to the persecuter of Christians.

Saul had never experienced such grace. He'd known ritual and rules. He'd tried to live up to expectations, but they had made him hard and angry. Now the grace of God was tenderizing his heart. Saul was still a gifted, determined, driven person, but the trajectory of his life radically changed. The shift didn't happen when he saw Jesus earlier in Jerusalem or at His trial. His heart wasn't melted when he watched Jesus suffer and die on the cross. It didn't change when he heard Stephen's message and watched him trust Jesus in his final breath. Saul's heart was transformed only when he encountered Jesus, was humbled by His power, and was reshaped by His love. During those three days of silence and darkness, God closed all the programs in Saul's mind and heart so He could reboot him.

God also transformed the road Saul and his men were traveling on. Saul had intended it as a highway of death, but it became a path to new life. He had intended to capture men and women in Damascus, but on the way, Jesus captured him. Before Saul saw the light, he thought he was doing God's will, but it was Satan's work. Now Jesus was preparing him to devote his considerable skills and knowledge to an entirely new purpose: to win people to Jesus and build them in their faith. Instead of arrogantly destroying Christ's kingdom, Saul would humbly serve it.

Sometimes I wonder if Luke had a smile on his face when he wrote parts of Acts. On several occasions, he describes events that are humorous in retrospect. One occurred when Paul talked so long that a young man named Eutychus drifted off to sleep and fell from a balcony to the floor. He was dead, but Paul prayed for him and restored him to life. No problem: Paul kept right on preaching till dawn! But that scene is years later in Luke's history (Acts 20:7-12).

When Saul was sitting in darkness in Damascus pondering his past, his present, and his future, God spoke through a vision to a believer there. This scene has a humorous twist, too. The Lord told Ananias, "Go to the house of Judas on Straight Street and ask for a man from Tarsus named Saul, for he is praying. In a vision he has seen a man named Ananias come and place his hands on him to restore his sight" (Acts 9:11-12).

The Christians in Damascus didn't have the Internet or smartphones, but they had heard Saul was on his way to their city. That wasn't good news! They were terrified! Ananias tried to talk Jesus out of the instructions: "Uh, Jesus, you may not know this, but this guy arrested a lot of people—*your* people—in Jerusalem. And now he's coming here. And, uh, he's not coming for a picnic. He's coming to capture and kill Christians, and Jesus, that includes me! Let me get this right: You want me to go to him and lay hands on him? Are you sure about this?"

I would love to have heard the tone in Jesus' voice when He answered Ananias' objections: "Go! This man is my chosen instrument to proclaim my name to the Gentiles and their kings and to the people of Israel. I will show him how much he must suffer for my name" (Acts 9:15-16). Ironically, the vicious man who caused Christians to suffer would suffer now for telling people about Jesus. Perhaps the assurance that Saul would suffer comforted Ananias.

The reluctant messenger found the house where Saul had been staying. He laid hands on him and prayed. Saul was filled with the Holy Spirit and scales fell from his eyes. He was baptized and ate. Now he was ready for a new life and a new career.

Much of the rest of Luke's story of the early church describes Saul's faithfulness to God's calling. He was sent to preach the gospel to the Gentiles, so he used his Roman name, Paul, for the rest of his life. He traveled from city to city, telling everyone about Christ and healing people, with decidedly mixed responses. Some trusted in Jesus, some walked away in confusion, and some tried to kill him. In every city, Paul experienced the entire spectrum of reactions as people considered his message about Jesus. His fierce dedication to eradicate the Christian faith was now pointed in the opposite direction. He gave everything he could, all the time, to honor the One who met him on the road that day.

His fierce dedication to eradicate the Christian faith was now pointed in the opposite direction. He gave everything he could, all the time, to honor the One who met him on the road that day.

Toward the end of his career, he explained the reasons for his intensity. He told church leaders from Ephesus, "I only know that in every city the Holy Spirit warns me that prison and hardships are facing me. However, I consider my life worth nothing to me; my only aim is to finish the race and complete the task the Lord Jesus has given me—the task of testifying to the good news of God's grace" (Acts 20:23-24).

In his book, *Crazy Love*, Francis Chan observed, "People who are *obsessed* with Jesus aren't consumed with their personal safety and comfort above all else. Obsessed people care more about God's kingdom coming to this earth than their own lives being shielded from pain or distress."[19] Paul was one of the people Chan described.

Paul's drive, however, was infused with something totally missing before he met Jesus: compassion. Even to the angry, critical, selfish Christians in Corinth, Paul reached out with tenderness. That group of believers had lots of problems, but Paul didn't blast them. Like Jesus tenderly reaching out to him on the Damascus road when he had been

---

19   Francis Chan, *Crazy Love* (David C. Cook: Colorado Springs, 2008), 133.

out of control, Paul wanted to melt the Corinthians' hearts with love. He explained the new power source in his life: "For Christ's love compels us, because we are convinced that one died for all, and therefore all died. And he died for all, that those who live should no longer live for themselves but for him who died for them and was raised again" (2 Corinthians 5:14-15).

Before his conversion, Paul had been powerful and wealthy. He had been at the top of his profession, and he won the admiration (and fear) of every person watching him. In the darkness of the days before Ananias showed up to pray for him, he realized none of that mattered at all. All the money, all the fame, all the comfort, and all the power are just a pipedream. Knowing, loving, and honoring Christ are all that matters. Paul explained this radical but reasonable perspective in many different letters, but none as clearly as the one he wrote to the Christians in Philippi:

> But whatever were gains to me I now consider loss for the sake of Christ. What is more, I consider everything a loss because of the surpassing worth of knowing Christ Jesus my Lord, for whose sake I have lost all things. I consider them garbage, that I may gain Christ and be found in him, not having a righteousness of my own that comes from the law, but that which is through faith in Christ—the righteousness that comes from God on the basis of faith. I want to know Christ—yes, to know the power of his resurrection and participation in his sufferings, becoming like him in his death (Philippians 3:7-10).

Everything people brag about—gold, clothes, cars, titles, prestige, acclaim, vacations, and anything else—is "garbage" next to the "surpassing worth of knowing Christ." We aren't acceptable because we have nice things, lofty titles, or power over others. And we're not valuable because we've followed a bunch of rules to prove we're good people. Ultimate value and God's approval come because Jesus has paid the price for us, and we've opened our hearts to receive His gift of grace. When that happens, everything changes: our motivations, our sense of security, our desire to obey, our purpose in life, and the source of our joy.

We learn to love people (even annoying ones) because we're amazed that Jesus loves rotten, selfish people like us. When we're filled with Christ's love, His presence begins to push out all the things that have cluttered our hearts for so long. When Christ fills us, we develop the quality that can only be created by the Spirit of God: humility.

The Roman Empire valued power and despised humility. Our culture isn't much different. But a mark of God's transforming power in Paul's life was that this arrogant, demanding, angry man became gentle and humble. Instead of abusing people, he began to serve them. Instead of intimidating them, he suffered for them. God ripped out the old hard drive and replaced it with a new one. If God could work this miracle in Paul's hard heart, He can do it in anyone.

> For three days, Paul lived in a tomb of darkness, and then he came to life and light with a new purpose.

REBOOTING US

Paul's experience on the road to Damascus was a type of death and resurrection. Everything he had known and believed died in the bright light of Jesus' presence. For three days, Paul lived in a tomb of darkness, and then he came to life and light with a new purpose. Jesus said that a plant can't germinate and grow unless the seed is put into the ground.

This principle is true for many aspects of life, including our relationship with Christ. We have to die to the old nature, the old values and habits that seemed so right. We can't recreate ourselves. Every aspect of the transformation from death to life is the work of God's Spirit. Our task is to recognize Him and believe.

Paul's response to Jesus is a model for us. As we look at his life, we learn crucial spiritual lessons.

Don't miss God's signals.

People experience difficulties, and they often remark, "I don't know why I didn't see it coming. Looking back, the signs were everywhere." We see this repeated on the news, and we hear it in our neighborhoods. Wisdom isn't the ability to know everything, but wise people notice signs and ask, "What does this mean? How should I respond to this?" For most of us, spiritual wisdom is the product of many years of experience. Over time, we learn to see the signals God gives us so we can make better choices.

Some people, however, seldom if ever see the signs. They continue to commit adultery even though their deceit is ruining their relationships with their spouse and kids. They keep speeding even though they've been stopped several times and risk losing their license. They don't exercise, and they wonder why they're flabby, out of breath, and gaining weight. The list is almost endless. Some of us just don't notice the connection between cause and effect!

God gives us lots of signals. Our task is to notice them. We may get a wakeup call from a doctor, a friend, a pastor, an employer, or a child. We may read the Scriptures and the Holy Spirit gives us illumination to understand how a truth can change our direction. We may pray and sense the Spirit's nudge to tell someone about Jesus, forgive a person who hurt us, or change a bad habit.

All difficult circumstances are road signs, but we have to learn to read them correctly. Some of them tell us, "You're on the wrong road. Go back and take a different path." Some say, "You're on the right road, but you need to slow down and take others with you." Many signs are corrective. Sometimes, though, God wants us to know that until we see Him face to face, we'll experience difficulties—and the signs remind us that He's always with us.

Roadblocks and road signs cause us to ask, "What's going on here?" We need to carefully analyze our motives, our attitudes, our behavior, and our words. Are we on a path that will harm people with our demands and anger? Is our tenacity and drive under the control of the Spirit? Do we display a beautiful blend of humility and boldness? Do we truly delight in God, or are we just going through the motions? Good questions and an honest heart enable us to read the signs more accurately.

Value the delays.

Only a generation or two ago, people understood the process of change and growth. Many people still lived on farms, and they experienced the seasons of plowing, planting, growing, and harvesting their crops. They weren't shocked when they went through winters when nothing seemed to grow. They expected those seasons. During the short days and long nights, they repaired tractors, sewed clothes, and got ready for the spring planting. Our culture, however, expects instant answers and immediate gratification. We demand a perpetual summer of abundance. Few of us value winters of delay that can be the source of our greatest spiritual insights.

If God had restored Paul's sight immediately, I doubt that driven man would have reflected as deeply as he did during the three days of

Delays aren't curses; they're God's "time out" to give us the opportunity to listen to Him.

waiting. Delays aren't curses; they're God's "time out" to give us the opportunity to listen to Him. In our day, people believe they have to be "on" all the time. They use email, Facebook, and Twitter to keep track of friends (and people they'll never know). They text and email incessantly. They fill their time with video games and television. Any "empty time" feels wrong! But always being attached to electronics devastates our spiritual lives. We need to recapture the spiritual disciplines of silence and solitude, or at least, we need to turn off all our devices for a half hour (at least) each day so we can have clarity to think and pray.

Waiting on the Lord for answers isn't wasted time. God uses such time to draw us deeper into our relationship with Him, to purify our motives, or redirect us. Many times I have looked back and realized I would have made a big mistake if I'd plowed through with a decision. Thankfully, God used a long delay to give me insight about the situation or people, and to provide more resources.

Realize suffering produces credibility.

People are watching us. They want to see if this Jesus we claim to know has actually made a difference in our lives. They're looking to see if we've really changed. Do we react in anger like we used to? Are we defensive or withdrawn when things don't go our way? Are we willing to overlook offenses and forgive those who hurt us?

People in the early church had every reason to be skeptical of Paul. Some of their friends and family members had been victims of his attacks. Then, when some church leaders claimed he'd changed, could they be sure of it? The only way to find out was to see if he was willing to put it all on the line for Jesus. Was Paul willing to suffer? If so, how far would he go?

The only way for Paul to change his reputation as a persecuter was to suffer for Christ as a victim of ridicule and abuse. As soon as he regained his sight and his strength, he went into the synagogue in Damascus to preach. The people who heard him that day were shocked when he proclaimed Jesus as Lord! After the message, he argued with the leading Jews to prove his point. Almost immediately, they hatched a plot to kill him. He had to escape by being lowered in a basket from a window in the city wall (Acts 9:23-25).

That was just the beginning. Many years later when the Christians in Corinth questioned his credibility, Paul had an answer for them. He gave them a catalog of his suffering for the cause of Christ:

I have worked much harder, been in prison more frequently, been flogged more severely, and been exposed to death again and again. Five times I received from the Jews the forty lashes minus one. Three times I was beaten with rods, once I was pelted with stones, three times I was shipwrecked, I spent a night and a day in the open sea, I have been constantly on the move. I have been in danger from rivers, in danger from bandits, in danger from my fellow Jews, in danger from Gentiles; in danger in the city, in danger in the country, in danger at sea; and in danger from false believers. I have labored and toiled and have often gone without sleep; I have known hunger and thirst and have often gone without food; I have been cold and naked. Besides everything else, I face daily the pressure of my concern for all the churches. Who is weak, and I do not feel weak? Who is led into sin, and I do not inwardly burn? (2 Corinthians 11:23-29)

People listen far more eagerly and intently if they know we've suffered—especially in the way they're suffering. A woman who has been diagnosed with breast cancer may appreciate a healthy person's kind words, but she feels deeply understood and encouraged when a breast cancer survivor steps into her life to share her story. Addicts don't pay much attention to well-meaning people who try to tell them to change, but they listen to recovering addicts who have struggled with the same compulsions and destructive behavior. Abuse victims are very skeptical of anyone who tries to tell them to "just get over it," but they may open their hearts to someone who has survived attacks and found a new life of security, hope, and peace. People who have lost their jobs or their homes feel more encouraged when they talk with others who have gone through the same painful experiences.

No matter what hardships we've faced, we have credibility if we've suffered, endured, and trusted God to give us healing and meaning.

Actually, we don't have to have experienced exactly the same problems to earn credibility. No matter what hardships we've faced, we have credibility if we've suffered, endured, and trusted God to give us healing and meaning. I know the struggles of growing up in a single mother's home in Humboldt Park in Chicago. I know the twisted minds and savage destruction caused by gangs. The pain and healing I've experienced gives me credibility to reach out to help people who struggle with problems I've never experienced, such as prostitutes and drug addicts.

No one signs up to suffer unless he has a sadomasochistic complex, but it's part of God's path for every believer. We may not suffer the same way as others we know, but we can be sure it's coming. If we try to avoid it, we'll miss out on an opportunity to learn. If we try to get it over too soon, we short-circuit God's desire to teach us deep, lasting lessons. But if we trust God through it, we become wiser, more compassionate people—and we reflect a little more of the heart of Christ.

LEADING WITH GRACE

Billy was born to be a leader. His desire to lead started at a young age. He went from being an altar boy to joining the church youth club and the high school letterman club. He was the founding member of an African-American fraternity in college and he wasn't even African-American. Billy's drive to lead compelled him to push through any obstacles. When he focused his mind on something, everything else vaporized. As a young man, he poured most of his time and energy into community activism—so much so that he was kicked out of college for failing grades. That didn't stop him from chasing his dreams and finishing college.

Sometimes you're on a mission to pursue your purpose in life, and you realize you've taken a wrong turn that's leading you nowhere. No matter how much fame, fortune, and education you may have, you can still hit a plateau or glass ceiling where you stop advancing. You realize that you've lost sight of what's most important—your relationship with God. You've taken yourself as far as you can go from an earthly perspective. Now it's time to let God lead you where you never dreamed of—to reach your divinely ordained full potential.

When Billy surrendered his heart, life, and dreams to God, he no longer allowed others to control his choices. He trusted God with all his heart. He no longer felt like Saul, but more like a transformed Paul. He learned about true leadership, and he teaches those powerful spiritual truths at our church's Men's Retreat. He learned that leaders must have the courage to change. He teaches other men that embracing the truth gives them the courage to express their convictions and press through expected obstacles.

A godly leader always takes the narrow road and inspires others to do the right thing. Leaders with a godly vision and unshakeable faith must exhibit humility and passionately pursue their mission.

Once you've awakened from a self-induced spiritual slumber and found your purpose, you must act on it, shed the heavy weights from your life that hold you back, and lastly but most importantly, put on Christ. He's our strength to press on and fulfill the purposes God has for our lives.

CONSIDER THIS...

1. What are some ways people try to control others and situations when they feel threatened?

2. What are some ways God gets people's attention? How did He get yours?

3. What signs does God give us? Which ones has He given you in the past year or so? How did you respond?

4. Are you too plugged into your electronics? What difference does it
   (or would it) make for you to build some quiet time into your life
   for reflection and prayer?

5. Who are some people whose suffering has earned credibility with
   you and others around you? Are you earning credibility by going
   through suffering with grace and peace? Explain your answer.

9   Give Your Best

You were made by God and for God, and until you understand that, life will never make sense.

—*Rick Warren*

Stephanie was in her first year of high school, but she had already suffered enough trouble for a lifetime. Her mother, Miriam, had been a drug addict since Stephanie was a little girl. Miriam's life now revolved entirely around crack, weed, and alcohol. She lived to get high. She stole to get a hit, sold drugs to make more money, and spent almost every dime on drugs. Stephanie and her two brothers were taken away from Miriam when they were young and were raised by their maternal grandmother.

Stephanie never respected her mother. She would see her mother on the streets, high. She knew that classmates from school would sell her mother drugs. They called her *druggie*. The summer before her first year in high school Stephanie became sexually active. She was trying to feel loved. She wanted to belong to somebody, and sex felt like love. One of her two brothers started taking ecstasy and was in and out of mental facilities. Stephanie never knew if her mother was coming home—and she wasn't sure she even wanted her to come home.

At one time in her life Miriam had been a hardworking mother who attended PTA meetings. Her life began to deteriorate when her brother introduced her to crack cocaine. In a six-month span, she lost everything: her kids, her job, her home, her money, and 60 pounds. She ran with the wrong people on the streets and spent two years in prison. Once she was raped at gunpoint. In desperation she tried to commit suicide six times, but every attempt failed. She tried every rehab and detox center in Chicago and even signed herself into mental facilities eighteen times over the course of two and half years. Nothing worked.

One New Year's Eve, Miriam ran into our church high and drunk, and one of the female pastors prayed with her while everyone else was celebrating the new year. Other female pastors followed up with visits to her home. During one such visit, Miriam told Pastor Alice, "I've tried everything." Pastor Alice responded, "Have you tried Jesus Christ?" That question stunned Miriam, and she answered, "No." Pastor Alice said, "Then you haven't tried everything."

That encounter shook Miriam to the core. Our pastors invited her to consider going through the program at the Chicago Dream Center and the farm for addicts and prostitutes. She agreed to go. There she met other women who were just like her—just as broken, just as afraid, and just as hopeful that this might be the answer they'd been looking for. She heard the message of grace from every angle, and God opened her heart to trust in Jesus. Week after week at both the Chicago Dream Center and the farm, she studied her Bible, asked plenty of questions, and discovered a new way to live.

As Miriam's mind cleared, she realized how deeply she had wounded her children. She couldn't wait to talk to them, ask for their forgiveness, and begin a new life with them—if they were willing to take steps to trust her again. At first Stephanie and her siblings were very skeptical. Miriam had made hundreds of promises over the years, but she had broken every one of them. Would this just be the next one in the line? Miriam understood that she was starting from way behind zero. Trust couldn't be earned with a word. She had to show them she had really changed.

> Miriam understood that she was starting from way behind zero. Trust couldn't be earned with a word. She had to show them she had really changed.

The months at the farm went by rapidly. When Miriam graduated, Stephanie and her brothers Ray and Robert came for the ceremony. There they heard the message of Christ. Within a few weeks, the changes in Miriam's life—her honesty, humility, and integrity—won their hearts. Stephanie and Robert wanted to experience the forgiveness and purpose they saw in their mother. They both came to Christ. Miriam's mother and three cousins also trusted in Jesus soon after they saw the unmistakable miracle of Miriam's transformation.

Stephanie's story is every bit as dramatic as Miriam's. In response to the change she saw in her mother, Stephanie found the courage to carve out a new direction in her life. She was thrilled that God had rescued her mother, and now He had rescued her and others in their family. When Stephanie came to church, the look on her face showed she was pouring out her heart in praise to God. Her worship wasn't superficial, and it wasn't routine. It was a heartfelt expression of the deepest joy and thankfulness.

The young girl had found what she had always been searching to find: love, meaning, and purpose. She was still in high school, and she got involved in all kinds of outreaches to kids who were as lost as she had been only months before. She wanted her life to count for Christ.

After she graduated, she participated in our discipleship program, Chicago Master's Commission. Seven years to the day that Miriam ran into the church on New Year's Eve, her daughter Stephanie was anointed as a minister. Stephanie is now serving as the host pastor of our church plant in Camden, New Jersey. She is giving her very best to God, not out of guilt, but from a heart steeped in gratitude.

When I ask people to serve, Stephanie and Miriam are the first ones to volunteer. When someone has a need, they're the first ones to give. When they notice someone in trouble, they're the first to step in to help. If you met these two women today, you'd see the biggest smiles on the planet. They know where they've come from, and they realize what God has done for them.

POURED OUT

When we picture Jesus in the Gospels, we often think of Him surrounded by twelve men. They were certainly there, but they were only part of a much bigger circle. At times in His ministry, a large entourage of men and women joined the twelve disciples in following Jesus from town to town. They were thrilled to hear Him teach, but probably more, they loved to get near Him and experience His love. Three people who became close friends of Jesus lived in Bethany, a small town near Jerusalem. They were Lazarus and his sisters, Mary and Martha.

One of the most poignant stories in John's account of Christ's life occurred outside their town. Lazarus became deathly sick, but Jesus was miles away. The sisters sent for Him because they were sure He could heal their brother. They'd seen Him perform many miracles—surely He could heal Lazarus, too. But Jesus didn't come. The days passed, Lazarus got sicker, and then . . . he died. Four days later, Jesus showed up. The sisters poured out their disappointment and heartache to Him, and He wept with them.

Then, without fanfare, Jesus called Lazarus's name and raised him from the tomb. We can imagine the immeasurable thrill these sisters felt when their brother stumbled out of the darkness wrapped in grave clothes! (Just imagine what would have happened if Jesus hadn't called Lazarus by name. When He said, "Come out," every dead person in the cemetery would have walked out into the light!)

A few days later, the sisters threw a party to celebrate. Jesus had solemnly warned everyone many times that He was on His way to Jerusalem for a divine purpose: to suffer and die for the sins of the world. His men didn't understand, but Mary did. She instinctively realized that the day of the party was sandwiched between two deaths: of Lazarus and Jesus. Her overwhelming joy of seeing her brother being restored to life was tempered by the painful reality that her dear friend Jesus was going to be killed. The party was held only a few days before Passover. For Him the end was very near.

At banquets and special dinners in the culture of first century Palestine, guests reclined on the floor with their heads near the table. They often rested their heads on one hand and ate with the other. At this dinner, the unimaginable was happening: Lazarus was there eating with everyone! Just a few days earlier, he had been as lifeless as a stone, but now he was laughing and talking. (What stories did he tell about the four days he was dead? That's way beyond a *near-death* experience. It was a *very dead* experience!) John was there, and he tells us what happened: "Then Mary took about a pint of pure nard, an expensive perfume; she poured it on Jesus' feet and wiped his feet with her hair. And the house was filled with the fragrance of the perfume" (John 12:3).

Nard was one of the most precious and expensive ointments in the Roman world. It was imported from northern India and used by the Romans and Jews to anoint the heads of honored people. It was also used in funerals. It was a particularly lovely perfume. Even a small drop of it would fill a room with a beautiful fragrance and waft through the windows to the streets outside. Mary used a full pint! It had been kept in an alabaster jar (Mark 14:3), which may have been even more valuable than the nard inside. In an unusual display of extravagance, she broke the jar and poured out all the contents on Jesus feet.

Normally, only the lowest servant washed a guest's feet, but Mary showed selfless humility by taking down her hair to wipe Jesus' feet. In their culture, women rarely unbound their hair in public. Then as now, a woman's hair was an important part of her beauty and her identity. Wiping the perfume on Jesus' feet with her hair showed Mary was using every ounce of her beauty to communicate her affection for Jesus. (Mark says she also anointed His head with the perfume.)

The house was filled with the wonderful aroma, and the people understood Mary was showing Jesus how much she loved Him. Everyone understood—except Judas. As Mary's outpouring of gratitude and love warmed all other hearts, Judas turned to someone and growled, "Why wasn't this perfume sold and the money given to the poor? It was worth a year's wages" (Mark 14:5). This, John explains, wasn't because he loved the poor and wanted to save the money to help them. He was the treasurer of the group, and a thief (John 12:6). If Mary had given him the jar of nard, he could have sold it and pocketed the cash.

Judas's remark was either loud and obnoxious or a stage whisper because everyone heard him. Jesus corrected him, "Leave her alone. It was intended that she should save this perfume for the day of my burial. You will always have the poor among you, but you will not always have me" (Mark 14:6-7).

The contrast between Judas and Mary couldn't have been clearer. His heart wasn't moved by the miracle of raising Lazarus from the dead (or watching countless other miracles from a front-row seat). He was still as selfish as ever. Mary's heart had been broken, melted, and remolded with new appreciation for Jesus. She grasped the essence of worship: giving everything we are, everything we have, and everything we'll ever be to the One who is wor-

> She grasped the essence of worship: giving everything we are, everything we have, and everything we'll ever be to the One who is worthy of our ultimate devotion. She gave the best she had.

thy of our ultimate devotion. She gave the best she had. The value of the jar and nard was probably her life's savings, the equivalent of her 401k, her pension, and the jar of cash kept under the bed.

More than anyone at the table, Jesus understood what she was doing. He longed for someone to understand His mission and His heart. Mary did. She anointed Him for burial a week before He was falsely accused, tried in a mockery of justice, convicted, tortured, and executed in history's most brutal act of punishment. During all that time, the smell of the perfume on His skin never faded away. As He was arrested, He smelled it. When Judas kissed Jesus, he was reminded of Mary's devotion at the moment he betrayed the Lord of life. When Jesus was beaten and whipped, His blood and sweat enhanced the fragrance and reminded Him of her love. As He suffered agony in the hours of death, the sweet smell of Mary's nard comforted Him. Others ran away, but she was there—at the cross, on His feet, and in His heart.

GIVING IT ALL

Mary's heart was so full of love and gratitude that she gladly poured out everything she had—the nard, the alabaster jar, her home, and her heart—to express her devotion to Jesus. She held nothing back. The fragrance of the perfume filled the air, and it lingered long after the party was over. Our expressions in worship—in church and everywhere we go—demonstrate the contents of our hearts.

The concept of expressing devotion isn't a modern phenomenon. From ancient times, people have looked for ways to tell God what's on their hearts. In the wilderness the children of Israel used the tabernacle to worship God. The brazen altar was outside the tent. Animals were slaughtered and sacrificed as symbols of the price of God's forgiveness and His covenant with His people.

When someone is slow-cooking barbecue, the wonderful smell spreads throughout the neighborhood. The aroma is delicious. In the same way, the smells from the brazen altar filled the camp and reminded the two million refugees from Egypt their God had paid the price for their freedom.

Inside the tent the altar of incense stood just outside the curtain to the Holy of Holies. It was constructed from acacia wood and overlaid in gold. In the morning and evening, the priests burned incense made from a blend of four precious spices: stacte, onycha, galbanum, and frankincense, and it burned throughout the day. The continual fragrance symbolized the prayers of the people going up to God all day, every day. It reminded them they could approach God with any problem or praise at any time.[20]

We don't worship in a tent today, and in fact, many Christians think worship is restricted to Sunday morning singing. It's not. The word comes from the old English word "worthship." It refers to something

---

20   "The Golden Altar of Incense of the Tabernacle," The Tabernacle Place, cited at www.the-tabernacle-place.com/tabernacle_articles/tabernacle_altar_of_incense.aspx, cited on 11/8/11.

that has surpassing value and is worthy of our affection and devotion. In response to the grace of God, we live for Him in every conversation, every choice, and every place—because He's worth it.

Paul captured this all-encompassing principle when he wrote the Christians in Rome: "Therefore, I urge you, brothers and sisters, in view of God's mercy, to offer your bodies as a living sacrifice, holy and pleasing to God—this is your true and proper worship. Do not conform to the pattern of this world, but be transformed by the renewing of your mind. Then you will be able to test and approve what God's will is—his good, pleasing and perfect will" (Romans 12:1-2). We can be living sacrifices of worship in the bedroom and the boardroom, the closet and the field, the classroom and the streets.

> We can be living sacrifices of worship in the bedroom and the boardroom, the closet and the field, the classroom and the streets.

Let's look at some lessons we learn from Mary's amazing devotion.

Develop a habit of being at Jesus' feet.

Uncommon devotion is a normal response to the greatness and grace of Christ. When Mary poured the costly nard on Jesus that day, she was doing what she had done many times before: she was living at the feet of Jesus. Months before when He came to their home for dinner, Martha complained that Mary was in the other room listening to Jesus instead of helping her cook dinner (Luke 10:38-42). A few days before when Jesus finally showed up at Lazarus's tomb, Mary was at Jesus' feet in her grief. Now she was at His feet again, but this time with a heart overflowing with thankfulness and praise. Whether things were good or things were hard, Mary always found Jesus and fell at His feet in humble submission and affection.

Don't wait.

Mary had seen one of the greatest miracles in the ministry of Jesus. John's Gospel includes seven signs that prove Jesus is the promised Messiah. The resurrection of Lazarus is one of them. But Mary didn't wait for a miracle to express her devotion. She had already expressed her love for Him before the miracle and the celebration. In the same way, some of us have lost jobs, had homes taken away in foreclosure, suffered health problems, seen marriages crumble, or watched children throw their lives away. Do we fall at Jesus' feet in those difficult times, or do we turn our backs on Him and walk away? Mary never walked away.

Also, Mary didn't delay her expression of gratitude until she had two jars of nard or Jesus performed another miracle. She instinctively understood that *now* was the time to honor Jesus. He affirmed her decision when He told Judas and the others, "You always have the poor, but you don't always have me." The implication was this: "If you don't pour out your hearts to Me now, soon it will be too late."

Give your best.

If we're just going through the motions of our Christian faith, we'll have sticky hands. We hang on to the things that are valuable, and we give God our castoffs and second best. When we praise Him, we hold back. When the Scriptures are taught, our minds drift to things we'd rather be doing. When the offering plate passes by, we think of all the ways we could use the money, so we give only enough to soothe our guilt.

Five centuries before Christ, the prophet Malachi got a word from God that speaks powerfully of the contrast between Mary and those who give as little as possible. God told His people, " 'My name will be great among the nations, from where the sun rises to where it sets. In every place incense and pure offerings will be brought to me, because

my name will be great among the nations,' says the LORD Almighty"
(Malachi 1:11).

God referred to the smells of the two altars in the temple, the brazen altar and the altar of incense. The fragrant smoke ascending from
these offerings shout that His name is great throughout the world! The
people, though, didn't get it. Their devotion was half-hearted. They held
back, and they gave far less than their best. God told them,

> "When you bring injured, lame or diseased animals and offer
> them as sacrifices, should I accept them from your hands?"
> says the LORD. "Cursed is the cheat who has an acceptable
> male in his flock and vows to give it, but then sacrifices a blem-
> ished animal to the Lord. For I am a great king," says the LORD
> Almighty, "and my name is to be feared among the nations"
> (Malachi 1:13-14).

Today we don't bring sheep and
goats to church to put in the offering plate—not in Chicago, anyway.
We aren't tempted to give God blind
sheep and lame goats, but we commit the same offense when we're
tempted to give Him less than our
best. If our minds are fixed on the
things we want, we'll cling to every penny so we can spend it on ourselves. If our hearts are filled with worry, we'll hold onto our money
because we're afraid we won't have enough. We'll guard our time, our
talents, and other treasures to keep God from getting too much from us.
However, if we realize we serve a great King, the sovereign Lord of the

> We aren't tempted to give God blind sheep and lame goats, but we commit the same offense when we're tempted to give Him less than our best.

universe and the Savior of mankind, our hearts will be filled with His love, and our hands will be open. We won't see how *little* we can give and get away with it; we'll see *how much* we can give. That's what Mary did, and she delighted Jesus' heart.

Expect criticism.

Selfless devotion, though, inevitably causes the Judases around us to be critical. When we gladly give our time and our resources to God and His cause, they grumble, "What a waste!" When we raise our hands in praise and tears of joy stream down our cheeks, they sneer, "It's just a show." We can't make them feel what we feel, just as Mary's wonderful example was completely lost on Judas. But Jesus noticed, and He treasured her expression of love. He defended her: "Leave her alone." He says the same thing about us today when others criticize us for being too sold out, too committed, and too passionate about Him.

Enjoy Jesus' smile.

The text doesn't describe the look on Jesus' face when Mary shocked the guests by breaking the expensive alabaster jar and pouring out the costly perfume on Jesus, but it's easy to imagine Him with a huge smile. He already had given so much, and He was about to give everything, but most people didn't understand Him or His mission. He must have been deeply moved by Mary's extravagant display of love. When Judas attacked her motives, she may have recoiled, but then she heard Jesus rebuke him. Jesus' defense of Mary confirmed His appreciation for her at that vulnerable moment.

When we sing with all our hearts, pray with expectancy, give gladly and generously, and love others the way Jesus loves us, we can sense Jesus' smile, too. He's thrilled when we act like Mary and go out of our way to show Him how much we love Him. Those kinds of displays are never stale. When a young couple in love wants to show their affection for each other, they come up with all kinds of creative expressions. They think for hours about how to delight the one they love. In the same way, when we genuinely love Jesus, we think, pray, and plan how to show Him our devotion. And when we pour ourselves out, we enjoy it as much as He does. That's the nature of love.

> When we sing with all our hearts, pray with expectancy, give gladly and generously, and love others the way Jesus loves us, we can sense Jesus' smile, too.

Remember the cost.

Mary's anointing that day wasn't just a haphazard act. Perhaps more than anyone else, she understood that the Jesus was going to die, and she was preparing Him for His burial. As the end approached, James and John struggled for power, Judas plotted to betray Jesus, and Peter made empty promises. Others lost their way, but Mary was fixed on the reason Jesus stepped out of heaven and came to earth: to be a ransom for many. During the difficult week before the Passover and the crucifixion, the smell of perfume on Jesus' body reminded Him of her love—and it reminded everyone else that at least someone understood who He was and what He came to do. Today we have the account of Mary's explosion of devotion as a reminder of the cost Jesus paid and our only appropriate response—giving ourselves unreservedly to Him.

EVEN ME

If we demand that God make things perfect in our lives before we love Him and trust Him, our hearts will shrink and our joy will fade.

We're fallen people who live in a fallen world. Jesus said we'll always experience difficulties, but He'll never leave us.

When I think about God's grace in my life, I'm amazed that He rescued me from a difficult home environment. I could have wallowed in despair and anger my whole life, but Jesus stepped in and saved me. He has worked the miracle of grace in the lives of my brothers and sisters, and He lets me have a front row seat to watch His power and love transform people in our community and around the world. I see individuals changed and families restored. I watch as God infuses hope and purpose into people who had been wandering aimlessly for years. I'm amazed that He's doing so much in so many people all around me, and I get to be part of it all. It's easy to sit at His feet with a heart full of contentment and gratitude. It's only right to kneel down and pour out my heart to express my worship and thanks. The only reasonable response is to live every minute to please Him.

Luke describes another scene in Jesus' life when a woman anointed Him with costly perfume. This time the woman was a prostitute who had been touched by Jesus' forgiving love. In fact, she was so moved that she barged into a dinner party hosted by one of her fiercest critics. Nothing could stop her from thanking Jesus! At the end of the party, Jesus explained to the resentful host, "I tell you, her many sins have been forgiven—for she loved much. But he who has been forgiven little loves little" (Luke 7:47).

We'll barge into any situation to insist on expressing our love for Him—even if some criticize us. Nothing matters but Jesus. He means everything.

Do you love Jesus only a little? Do you give him half-hearted praise and hoard all the gifts He's given you? If you're guarded in your relationship with Him, maybe you haven't experienced His forgiveness very deeply. When you and I are overwhelmed with the depth of our sins and the height of His grace, we'll be overcome with gratitude. We'll barge into any situation to insist on expressing our love for Him—even if some criticize us. Nothing matters but Jesus. He means everything.

To have Mary's amazing heart of devotion for Christ, we have to hold other things with a looser grip. Corrie Ten Boom, a Dutch Christian who helped Jews escape the Holocaust during World War II, and a survivor herself, often said, "Hold loosely to the things of this life, so that if God requires them of you, it will be easy to let them go."

Will you come with me to follow Mary's example? Will you join me in being overwhelmed with the love of Christ so we are absolutely devoted to Him?

A song by Anthony Gomez captures the heart of worship:

I'll hold nothing back. Every part of me belongs to you.
I'll hold nothing back. What you ask of me I will do.
I'll hold nothing back, so my life may bring you glory. Oh,
It's because of you that I am free, so I . . .
I'll hold nothing back.[21]

Let's make this song our prayer.

---

21 "I'll Hold Nothing Back," Music and lyrics by Anthony Gomez.

CONSIDER THIS...

1. When was a time when you felt overwhelmed with the greatness and grace of Jesus? How did you respond to show your gratitude?

2. What are some reasons people hold back and give less than their best? What do they value more? How do they justify their half-heartedness?

3. When you see people who express their love for Jesus in singing, giving, sharing, or serving, are you skeptical or inspired? Explain your answer.

4. Is there anything holding you back from full, glad devotion to Jesus? If so, what is it? (Think and pray through the song at the end of the chapter.)

5. Take a few minutes now to talk to Jesus about how you feel about Him.

6. What are the two or three most important principles you'll apply from this book?

About the Author

Wilfredo De Jesús is the Senior Pastor of New Life Covenant Ministries. Under his visionary leadership, New Life has become the largest Assemblies of God church in the United States. Through his ministry, Reverend De Jesús (or Pastor Choco as he is better known) impacts thousands of individuals in the Chicago area and around the world each week.

Wilfredo was born and raised in the Humboldt Park area. He grew up in a cultural and political climate that had the odds stacked against him. However, at the young age of fourteen, when he held a maintenance position at a small local church for a summer youth employment program, he encountered Jesus as his Lord and Savior.

De Jesús dedicated himself to that local church, called Templo Palestina (Palestine Christian Temple). In 1992, he became an administrative assistant at the church. From 1998 to 2000, he held two major positions, one as Assistant Pastor at Templo Palestina and the other as the Executive Assistant to the CEO of the Chicago Public Schools.

Twenty years after he first set foot in Templo Palestina, Alfredo was appointed the senior pastor. Giving the church a new name and a fresh vision, God began to expand the ministry from a weekly attendance of 120 to over 5,000 locally and more than 12,000 in both Spanish and

English under a vast ministry umbrella. New Life has planted churches across the city (Pilsen and Oakwood) and around the world (Camden, New Jersey, and Chimbote, Peru). Several other churches have come under Alfredo's ministry leadership network to advance the gospel and reach the lost.

De Jesús has extended the church beyond its four walls into the community. Outside of the church's thriving youth group and children's ministry, New Life operates an affordable private school (Salem Christian School), a free residential program for at-risk youth (Axis Teen Center), and an intensive discipleship program for college age students (Chicago Master's Commission). Under De Jesús' direction, New Life has launched several non-profit entities that help the "least of these": the Chicago Dream Center, New Life Family Services, Camden Dream Center, and New Life Foundation are among over 130 ministries under the New Life umbrella. These organizations operate multi-faceted programs including food and clothing pantries, transitional shelters, residential recovery and job training, mobile soup kitchens for the homeless and shut-ins, gang and at risk youth intervention, and human trafficking advocacy.

While serving in ministry, Wilfredo received a BA in communications from Trinity University and an MA in Christian ministries from North Park Theological Seminary. De Jesús is the Vice President of Social Justice for the nation's largest Hispanic Christian organization, The National Hispanic Christian Leadership Conference, which serves 18,000 churches and close to fifteen million born-again Christians. From 2004–2010, De Jesús served as a commissioner on the Chicago Zoning Board of Appeals. Widely sought after as a motivational speaker, he currently resides in Chicago with his wife, Elizabeth, and their three children, Alexandra, Yesenia, and Wilfredo, Jr.

Using *Amazing Faith* in Classes and Groups

This book is designed for individual study, small groups, and classes. The best way to absorb and apply these principles is for each person to individually study and answer the questions at the end of each chapter then to discuss them in either a class or a group environment.

Each chapter's questions are designed to promote reflection, application, and discussion. Order enough copies of the book for each person to have a copy. For couples, encourage both to have their own book so they can record their individual reflections.

A recommended schedule for a small group or class might be:

Week 1: Introduce the material. As a group leader, tell your story of finding and fulfilling God's dream, share your hopes for the group, and provide books for each person. Encourage people to read the assigned chapter each week and answer the questions.

Weeks 2–10: Each week, introduce the topic for the week and share a story of how God has used the principles in your life. In small groups, lead people through a discussion of the questions at the end of the chapter. In classes, teach the principles in each chapter, use personal illustrations, and invite discussion.

PERSONALIZE EACH LESSON

Don't feel pressured to cover every question in your group discussions. Pick out three or four that had the biggest impact on you, and focus on those, or ask people in the group to share their responses to the questions that meant the most to them that week.

Make sure you personalize the principles and applications. At least once in each group meeting, add your own story to illustrate a particular point.

Make the Scriptures come alive. Far too often, we read the Bible like it's a phone book, with little or no emotion. Paint a vivid picture for people. Provide insights about the context of people's encounters with God, and help those in your class or group sense the emotions of specific people in each scene.

FOCUS ON APPLICATION

The questions at the end of each chapter and your encouragement to group members to be authentic will help your group take big steps to apply the principles they're learning. Share how you are applying the principles in particular chapters each week, and encourage them to take steps of growth, too.

THREE TYPES OF QUESTIONS

If you have led groups for a few years, you already understand the importance of using open questions to stimulate discussion. Three types of questions are *limiting, leading,* and *open.* Many of the questions at the end of each lesson are open questions.

Limiting questions focus on an obvious answer, such as, "What does Jesus call himself in John 10:11?" They don't stimulate reflection or discussion. If you want to use questions like these, follow them with thought-provoking, open questions.

Leading questions require the listener to guess what the leader has in mind, such as, "Why did Jesus use the metaphor of a shepherd in

John 10?" (He was probably alluding to a passage in Ezekiel, but many people don't know that.) The teacher who asks a leading question has a definite answer in mind. Instead of asking this kind of question, you should just teach the point and perhaps ask an open question about the point you have made.

Open questions usually don't have right or wrong answers. They stimulate thinking, and they are far less threatening because the person answering doesn't risk ridicule for being wrong. These questions often begin with "Why do you think...?" or "What are some reasons that...?" or "How would you have felt in that situation?"

PREPARATION

As you prepare to teach this material in a group or class, consider these steps:

1. Carefully and thoughtfully read the book. Make notes, highlight key sections, quotes, or stories, and complete the reflection section at the end of each day's chapter. This will familiarize you with the entire scope of the content.

2. As you prepare for each week's class or group, read the corresponding chapter again and make additional notes.

3. Tailor the amount of content to the time allotted. You won't have time to cover all the questions, so pick the ones that are most pertinent.

4. Add your own stories to personalize the message and add impact.

5. Before and during your preparation, ask God to give you wisdom, clarity, and power. Trust Him to use your group to change people's lives.

6. Most people will get far more out of the group if they read the chapter and complete the reflection each week. Order books before the group or class begins or after the first week.

To Order More Copies

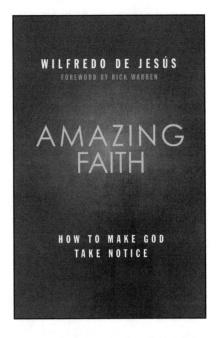

To order more copies of *Amazing Faith,* go to
www.influenceresources.com